Basics Series

CHANGE Basics

JEFFREY RUSSELL
LINDA RUSSELL

A Complete How-to Guide to Help You:

Introduce, Manage, and Lead Change

Reduce Resistance, Build Change Resilience

Implement a Solid 10-Step Action Plan

ASTD Press is an internationally renowned source of insightful and practical information on workplace learning and performance topics, including training basics, evaluation and return-on-investment (ROI), instructional systems development (ISD), e-learning, leadership, and career development.

Ordering information: Books published by ASTD Press can be purchased by visiting our Website at store.astd.org or by calling 800.628.2783 or 703.683.8100.

Library of Congress Control Number: 2006923212

ISBN-10: 1-56286-452-1
ISBN-13: 978-1-56286-452-1

Acquisitions and Development Editor: Mark Morrow
Copyeditor: Karen Eddleman
Interior Design and Production: Kathleen Schaner
Cover Design: Ana Ilieva
Cover Illustration: Paul Vismara

Printed by Victor Graphics, Inc., Baltimore, Maryland, www.victorgraphics.com.

Table of Contents

About the *Training Basics* Series

ASTD's *Training Basics* series recognizes and, in some ways, celebrates the fast-paced, ever-changing reality of organizations today. Jobs, roles, and expectations change quickly. One day you might be a network administrator or a process line manager, and the next day you might be asked to train 50 employees in basic computer skills or to instruct line workers in quality processes.

Where do you turn for help? The ASTD *Training Basics* series is designed to be your one-stop solution. The series takes a minimalist approach to your learning curve dilemma and presents only the information you need to be successful. Each book in the series guides you through key aspects of training: giving presentations, making the transition to the role of trainer, designing and delivering training, and evaluating training. The books in the series also include some advanced skills such as performance and basic business proficiencies.

The ASTD *Training Basics* series is the perfect tool for training and performance professionals looking for easy-to-understand materials that will prepare non-trainers to take on a training role. In addition, this series is the perfect reference tool for any trainer's bookshelf and a quick way to hone your existing skills. The titles in the series include:

- *Presentation Basics*
- *Trainer Basics*
- *Training Design Basics*
- *Facilitation Basics*
- *Communication Basics*
- *Performance Basics*
- *Evaluation Basics*
- *Needs Assessment Basics*
- *Return on Investment (ROI) Basics*
- *Organization Development Basics*
- *Coaching Basics*
- *Job Aids Basics*

Preface

Change is fundamental to everything in life. Whether it involves learning how to walk or stepping into the role of chief executive officer of a company, change defines every aspect of human beings' lives. Because of the central role that change plays in life, you'd think that everyone would be a master of it by adulthood. To the contrary, although most people survive the changes thrust upon them—or those they bring upon themselves—all those lessons learned are somehow forgotten when it's time to lead change in their own organizations.

In writing this book, we set out to provide a roadmap and guide to help those who want to lead and manage change in their organizations. The guidebook we created, *Change Basics,* offers a single point of reference that identifies the critical actions that leaders, managers, organization development professionals, and trainers should take to effect change in their organizations. We wanted to provide a simple, solution-based path to a successful change outcome. The work of a change leader is rarely easy, but we hope that *Change Basics* gives you the insight and direction you need to achieve your organizational transformational goals.

What's Inside This Book?

Change Basics offers you a single point of reference for understanding, managing, and leading change. Within these pages, you will find useful tools, tips, strategies, methods, and approaches that will help you know what works when it comes to the art of successfully introducing a change. We cut to the heart of the key issues you need to know and offer specific suggestions for actions and strategies that you and other change leaders can use to translate your vision for change into results.

In this book, you will learn about the nature of change and how it affects people. You'll explore the variety of forces that are driving change today, recognizing that every meaningful change experienced by organizations should be anchored to fundamental forces that are driving the change. We offer you tools for assessing organizational readiness for change and help you understand why people tend to resist change.

A central part of the book involves a powerful model that charts the change leader's path for introducing a change and provides a framework for understanding and responding to the emotional journey people follow when they are asked or compelled to change. Other key topics that we explore in this book include:

- the role of culture in introducing and managing change
- understanding and developing employee resilience in the face of change
- using appreciative inquiry to identify issues and organizational assets that will help facilitate the change
- the power of an effective communication strategy to support your change efforts
- a 10-step plan for developing and implementing a successful change initiative.

Icons to Guide You

This book has plenty to offer in the way of content that can help you every day. Some icons will alert you to key features of the book. Here are the ones you'll find throughout all of ASTD's *Training Basics* series:

What's Inside This Chapter?

Each chapter opens with a short summary that serves as a quick reference to the chapter contents. Use this section to identify the information in the chapter and, if you wish, skip ahead to the material that is most useful to you.

Think About This

These are helpful tips that you can put in your back pocket to pull out when needed as you prepare to implement a change initiative.

Basic Rules

These rules cut to the chase. They are unequivocal and important concepts or rules of thumb.

Noted

This icon flags sections that provide greater detail or an explanation about a concept or a principle. Sometimes it is also used for a short but productive tangent.

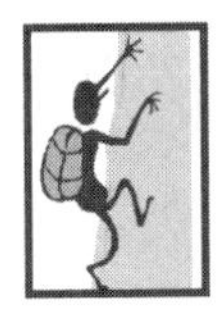

Getting It Done

The final section of each chapter supports your ability to take the content of that chapter and apply it to your situation. The focus of this section is mostly on thought problems and tools for understanding the content. Sometimes this section contains a list of questions for you to ponder, sometimes it is a self-assessment tool, and sometimes it is a list of action steps you can take to improve your skills and increase the chances for success.

Leading or Managing Change?

Do you lead change or do you manage it? What's the difference? Throughout this book, you'll see repeated references to "leading change" or "change leader." We use these terms purposefully. We want to convey the idea that leaders are those who drive change, who stir the pot, who envision an alternative reality to the present, who have a passion for a different future. Change leaders are the visionary drivers who literally take the lead and become a catalyst for making the change happen.

If you see what needs to change and are committed to inspiring others toward that vision, then you are a change leader. If you want to make sure that the change is implemented well, that the organization hits its targets, and that it gets the results that you are hoping for, then you are a change manager. If you are both driving the change and wanting to implement it effectively, then you are both a change leader and manager. Successful change initiatives require both leadership and management—just like successful organizations.

Although *Change Basics* uses the term "change leader" throughout, it provides models, methods, and tools for both the change leader and the manager. We acknowledge the dual role of both leading and managing change by providing the reader with opportunities to practice and apply tools and approaches from each discipline. Peter Drucker once said, "We are overmanaged and underled!" He argued that, as a society, we need to do more leading than managing; therefore, the focus in this book is on leading change.

Acknowledgments and Appreciations

This book couldn't have been written but for the lives of two very important people: our mothers. Linda's mother, Phyllis, and Jeff's mother, Flora Lou, have been living and breathing examples of adaptability and resilience. Each raised four headstrong children, each found ways to pay the bills and keep their families well fed, each dealt with loss with great dignity, and each always put the needs of family first. Both Flora Lou and Phyllis knew what they had to do to keep their families going and, when changes needed to be made, they were resourceful in knowing what needed to happen and how to make it happen.

Although Flora Lou passed on in 1998, her undaunted spirit and passion for life infuses everything we do. We have the good fortune of continuing to learn from Phyllis as she faces the world with determination and hope.

Thanks, Moms, for bringing us into the world and for steering us in the right direction. For us, you made everything happen!

Linda and Jeff Russell
May 2006

1

The Challenge of Change

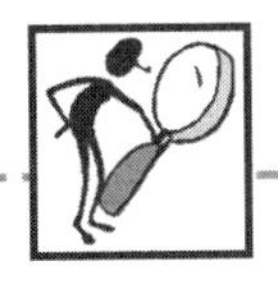

What's Inside This Chapter

In this chapter you'll learn about:

- Characteristics of change
- Common changes occurring in organizations today
- The implications of the sigmoid curve
- The key task of change leaders
- Your organization's potential change vulnerabilities.

The Paradox of Change

Despite the myriad books that discuss how difficult change is to implement—whether in people's lives or in organizations—in reality, change is an extraordinarily natural and normal practice that people embrace...when they want to. Conventional wisdom says that change is difficult. In some respects, that is true, particularly when change pushes people out of their comfort zones and compels them to move in directions that they don't think they want to go. In other respects, however, change is profoundly simple and easy to implement. When people are in the driver's seat of change, seeking out learning, a new direction, or a new opportunity, they actually view change as an ally to their personal success. It becomes the wellspring for growth and improvement.

Basic Rule 1

Change is a natural and normal part of everyday life. People embrace change on their own terms.

To demonstrate the truth of this, consider for a minute how your life would be different if, suddenly, you stopped changing. What if, by some twist of fate, you were caught in the "Twilight Zone" where change simply ceased to exist for you? In this extraordinary scenario, you would only interact with the same group of family, friends, and co-workers; you would live in the same house or apartment with the same furnishings for the rest of your life; you would be doing the same job, day in, day out; your children would never grow up; you would eat at the same restaurant with the same rude waiter; you would never read another book; you would never again experience wonder or awe; you would never experience a blazing scarlet sunset; your life would have no surprises; you would keep making the same mistakes again and again; and you would never learn anything new. You get the picture: Without change, life would be grindingly tedious and deadly.

Fortunately, change comes to the rescue. When people view change as an ally and partner, it provides the energy and zest that enables them to learn and grow, to become more effective in their personal and professional lives. When people instead only see change as a threat, they view it almost as an evil force that pushes them in directions that, they fear, will only bring loss, uncertainty, and confusion, and the disintegration of what they know and are comfortable with.

The paradox of change, the absurd contradiction of change, is that although change is the source of life energy, it is also a source of great stress and anxiety. The more that a coming change challenges people, the more that it moves them away from what they know, the greater the distress and anxiety they are likely to feel. The challenge for the change leader or organization development practitioner is to understand the paradox of change and its implications for how change is introduced and implemented in the organization.

The Nature of Change

Change, by its nature, destabilizes and disrupts the status quo. It breaks the linear continuity of life and, in doing so, moves people out of complacency and often into discomfort. This disruptive nature of change is true even for change that is viewed as positive and productive. Within this positive context, the change helps break people or organizations free from what was and is and enables them to move toward what they hope for.

Noted

Webster's dictionary defines change as "to make the form, content, or future course of something different from what it is, or from what it would be if left alone" and "to transform or convert." In both definitions, the heart of change is movement, transition, and discontinuity.

Although a given change may be necessary for survival or for growth and opportunity, it still tampers with something stable that had been carried along by momentum.

It is essential that you understand the paradoxical nature of change and its fundamental meaning so that you can manage and lead change effectively. You need to understand and appreciate the fact that change is second nature to most human beings, even when it disrupts their lives. When you approach organizational change from this perspective, you will be much more able to lead others through change and, consequently, manage and lead change initiatives in your organization more effectively. By drawing upon its paradoxical nature, you will be much more effective at developing successful strategies for introducing organizational change.

Basic Rule 2

The more disruptive a change is to the status quo, the greater it erodes people's individual capacities to envision their own futures.

Related to its paradoxical nature, two additional characteristics of change can have a significant influence on the success of your change initiatives (Russell & Russell, 1998):

1. Change introduces disruptions that can significantly diminish both an individual's and a group's capacities to envision a clear and positive future. The more disruptive a change is to the status quo, the greater it erodes people's capacity to envision the future, and the more likely it is that it will have a significantly negative effect upon individual and collective self-confidence, competence, morale, and self-esteem.
2. The path of any change is uncertain and unpredictable. As a leader of change, you might think you know where the change you are introducing will lead yourself and others, but there are always unintended consequences when you disrupt a stable system. As the Law of Unintended Consequences postulates, actions of people always have effects that are unanticipated or unintended. When you introduce a change, you may or may not get what you hoped for, but you will end up with consequences that you don't anticipate.

Basic Rule 3

The path of any change is uncertain and unpredictable.

Whether driven by the reactions of an organization's employees or customers, or its financial realities, competition, or other pressures, any change initiative must find a way to adjust for some hard organizational realities. Despite a change leader's efforts to think strategically and to manage the change process effectively, the path and destination of change are unknowable. Once begun, every change initiative follows its own path, meaning that people, other than the change leader, influence its future. Leading change successfully involves, at a minimum, staying deeply engaged throughout the change process by providing ongoing direction and by accommodating the ideas and insights of other stakeholders to shape the change as it evolves.

The unpredictable nature of change, of course, also has a profound effect upon those whose lives are affected directly by the change. Just when people think that

Noted

The Law of Unintended Consequences holds that all human actions have at least one unintended consequence, one that cannot be anticipated. Coined by sociologist Robert K. Merton, the law is at work wherever and whenever humans make decisions and take actions. An example of an unintended consequence: The U.S. government, through the Central Intelligence Agency, supported the work of Osama bin Laden and other radical Muslims in their fight against the Soviet occupation in Afghanistan. What they failed to anticipate was that these Islamic jihadists would have their own long-term agenda that eventually would be directed against the United States. Leaders who are most effective at managing a change initiative realize that the final results from a change effort could be considerably different from what they expected and hoped for.

they understand an impending change and make adjustments in their lives to the new direction, the path of change alters. Even if some of this redirection is due to their own influence (resistance or contributions to the change vision), the continuing evolution of the change has a tendency to sustain, if not increase, their anxiety, frustration, and anger.

It's clear, then, that an important challenge for change leaders is to recognize the inherent characteristics of change—its natural organic qualities, its potential for disruption, and its unknowable nature—and then to work with this nature rather than against it. When change leaders integrate these characteristics of change into their change management strategies, they are likely to experience less frustration and stress while increasing the chances that the change they promote will achieve the intended results for the organization and its stakeholders.

Our Changing Environment and the Work of the Change Leader

You don't have to look very far to see the challenges facing you as an organizational change leader. Although you might personally embrace the idea of change as natural and organic, the pace and complexity of the changes sweeping through the typical workplace can often be overwhelming. Table 1-1 highlights some common changes that are transforming organizations today.

Table 1-1. Common changes facing organizations today.

- The global marketplace and the competitive environment
- Greater diversity in the workforce
- Greater diversity in the customer base, leading to changing customer expectations and needs
- Instant global communication
- Telecommuting workers
- Transfer of jobs offshore to reduce costs of production
- Growth of Web-based transactions and commerce
- Six Sigma, ISO 9000 quality standards, and continuing pressure for quality
- Erosion of the social contract between employers and employees
- Retiring baby boomers
- Health-care costs spiraling upward
- Exponential growth of the Asian economies
- Erosion of public trust in business and government

Many of these changes are fast moving and most are occurring in conjunction with others. Some of these changes are clearly visible and have obvious implications and consequences; others are quieter and more subtle in their effects. Rarely are organizations experiencing a singular change. More typically, they experience a conflation of multiple changes occurring simultaneously. The pace and simultaneity of these convergent changes have their consequences—for you in your change agent role and for people at all levels of your organization.

Your personal response to these changes may range from leading a change because you recognize its value to working against a change when it threatens something you hold dear. Now, multiply your own responses, both positive and negative, by the number of people in your organization. You begin to see the enormity of the task in front of you.

The most important work you face as a change leader is to help build your organization's capacity to deeply understand, learn to embrace, and effectively respond to these changes. In times of crisis (often brought on by these changes), it's easy to get people's attention. The "Change or die!" mantra resonates. When, however, your company is doing well—when it has apparently successfully navigated through the stormy seas of change—it is often difficult to get people's attention. That is the paradox of success!

Think About This

The key challenges for an organizational manager or leader involve getting out in front of these changes, not being surprised when they occur, becoming a change agent or catalyst when necessary, and helping others move of their own free will to engage the changes directly. Change is inevitable. Guiding our organizations and its stakeholders toward growth in the face of these changes is not optional; it is the work of leaders to nudge people in the direction of growth.

Why Change Is Necessary (or the Paradox of Success)

In his 1993 book *The Paradox of Success,* author John O'Neil asserts that one of the reasons that some people fail as leaders is that their past and present success blinds them to their vulnerabilities and renders them all but incapable of sustaining the success that they are (for now) enjoying. What lies behind this failure? Whether due to hubris, ignorance of emerging issues, fatigue, or the circle of sycophants surrounding the leader who don't question his or her words, the leaders who fall prey to the paradox of success miss the early warning signs. They ignore the dissident and often discordant voices at the edge of their awareness. To their misfortune, the signs and voices that they push away carry with them the very information that they must know to stay on top of their game.

For successful leaders, the challenge of the paradox is to rise above self-satisfaction, realistically assess their capacities, and then take the steps they need to take to sustain their initial success. Learning from the paradox of success means that leaders must move away from a sense of complacency that can result from being at the top. They can do that through deep personal reflection, critical self-assessment, provocative questioning, challenging one's sense of self, and finally through personal growth and learning.

What has this to do with organizational change? Organizations, like leaders, experience their own paradox of success. When they achieve success, they are just as prone to slip into comfortable complacency. When something is working, the organizational culture says, why change it? If they're "best in class," why worry?

Jonas Salk (1973), the creator of the polio vaccine, offers a fascinating explanation of the natural origins of the paradox of success. Salk discovered through his work with biological systems that all natural systems have an innate, built-in growth or learning curve that explained the rise and fall of a species within the system. His research described the S-shaped or sigmoid curve (figure 1-1) that plotted the life and death cycle of every living system. He argued that, to survive over the long term, an individual species would need to change or learn a new adaptive behavior to escape disintegration—the disappearing, downward tail of the curve. Although previous researchers described this curve as a common characteristic in the natural world, Salk was the first to extrapolate the sigmoid curve to a new theory of adaptation and learning that applied to human systems, including organizations.

Figure 1-1. Salk's sigmoid curve for human systems.

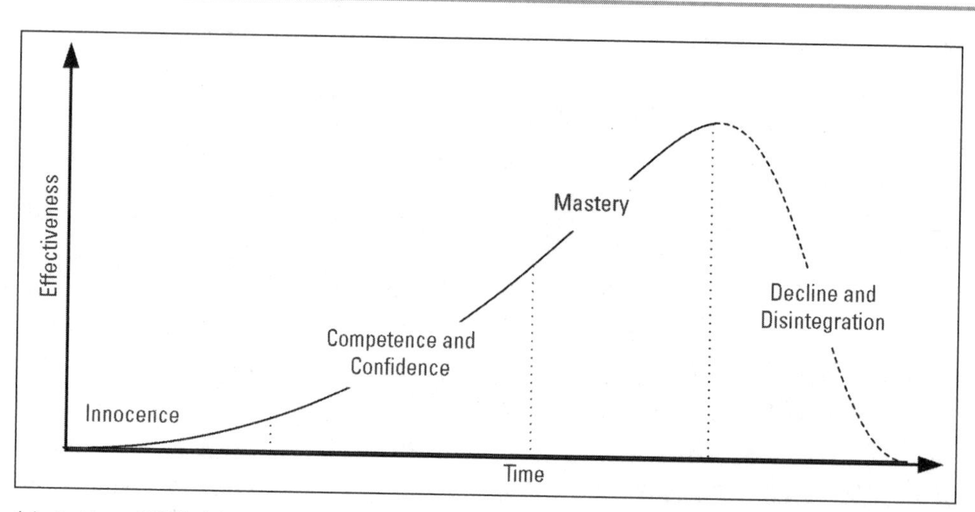

Adapted from O'Neil, John. (1993). *The Paradox of Success: When Winning at Work Means Losing at Life.* New York: Putnam and Sons, p. 125.

The far left end of the sigmoid curve, where performance and effectiveness are low, is labeled "innocence." In this phase of the curve, the new and emerging organization experiences considerable confusion and collective frustration as its leaders and staff members struggle with what works. This early stage, although infused with the positive energy of learning, is marked by repeated attempts, trials, and errors as the organization stumbles around in its search for best practices and successful performance. Over time, frustration yields to discovery as the organization begins to reflect upon and learn from its hits and misses. It scraps what doesn't work and builds on what does.

At the competence and confidence level of the curve, the pace of organizational learning accelerates as successful behaviors, structures, and patterns create a self-reinforcing positive feedback loop: success breeds success. The self-confidence of leaders and staff members pulls the organization steeply up the curve toward ever-higher levels of performance and effectiveness. The positive performance is reinforced by customers, investors, the industry, and other external voices that become ever more attracted to the organization's growing reputation for top-quality results.

The organization achieves optimal performance in a given environment as it reaches mastery. In this phase of the curve, the leaders and members of the organization feel a great sense of accomplishment and power. This citadel position is well deserved; the organization has struggled mightily as it has successfully overcome obstacles and, gradually, maximized its efforts, resulting in leading-edge performance.

Near the top of the curve, the pace and rate of learning, growth, and performance begin leveling off. Leaders and staff members enjoy the exhilaration of being at the top. The recognition, accolades, and financial rewards from the outside roll in, further reinforcing the organization's self-image of an organization that, it seems, can do no wrong. Therein lies the paradox of success. In mastery lie the seeds of the next phase: decline and disintegration.

Basic Rule 4

That which has made your organization successful today prevents it from being successful tomorrow. This is what O'Neil terms "the paradox of success."

Decline and disintegration evolve naturally out of mastery as the energy level and learning gradually decline and then rapidly disintegrate as the organization loses its edge. The decline results from a confluence of forces: a changing environment; fatigue brought on by the intensity of the organization's preceding efforts; the hubris and self-importance that say "we're the best"; and the resulting inability or unwillingness by leaders and staff members to see warning signs, to seek out contrarian and divergent perspectives, or to challenge their self-perception. Even the emptiness that is sometimes felt when a significant accomplishment has been realized moves an organization inexorably toward decline and disintegration.

It's not surprising that organizations would strive to maintain their mastery and the good feelings that arise from being at the top. What is surprising is that the desire to stay at mastery directly contributes to the erosion of the organization's effectiveness. Organizations attain mastery by achieving peak performance in a given environment. If the environment changes, however, while they cling to what is now a less relevant mastery, they lose their bearings and, eventually, their reputation. So, they hang their hats on what enabled them to be successful, but the hat rack is simply less relevant in the world, and they are less willing and able to embrace change.

Think About This

When U.S. President Abraham Lincoln rose to give his second annual address to Congress in December of 1862, the Civil War had worn on for more than 18 months and the Union Army had experienced significant defeats in fierce battles with the Confederate Army. The first part of his Emancipation Proclamation had been issued a couple months earlier. He challenged the Congress and the nation to meet the challenges ahead by thinking in new ways: "The dogmas of the quiet past are inadequate to the stormy present. The occasion is piled high with difficulty, and they must rise to the occasion. As our case is new, so they must think anew and act anew." Lincoln argued that the challenges of the future required the Union to move beyond its old conceptions of the way the world worked and to embrace a new reality with new ways of thinking and acting (Lincoln & Basler, 1953, p. 537).

Fortunately, there is a way out. Decline and disintegration are not inevitable. Salk proposed that at any time during mastery or during the rapid descent into decline and disintegration, a living system can pull itself out of its eroding performance by beginning a new learning curve. Figure 1-2 focuses on the mastery plateau of learning curve *A* and its relationship to the introduction of another learning curve, called learning curve *B*. The moment in time when this new learning curve begins is the "self-awareness" or simply the "awareness" point. This "aha!" moment occurs when the organization—through its leaders and staff members—becomes aware that it needs to change or face the stark consequences of decline and disintegration.

Figure 1-2. Embarking on a new learning curve.

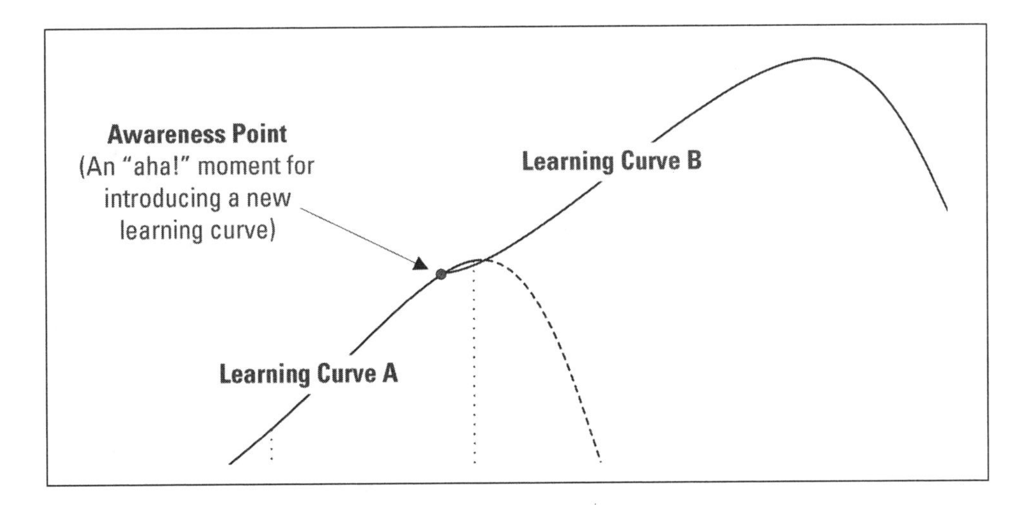

The good news with having an "aha!" moment is that it can occur at any point along the sigmoid curve. Although it is most useful to instigate organizational self-awareness as it achieves or nears mastery, such moments are possible even as the organization begins its descent into decline and disintegration. Any organization can pull itself out of a death spiral; it's never too late to begin a new learning curve. The sooner it does so, however, the fewer the immediate negative consequences and the more likely the organization can rebound and avoid disintegration.

The Task for Change Leaders

Reflecting upon the sigmoid curve, it's clear that one of the principal tasks for those who are leading or managing a change initiative is to help facilitate the organization's critical self-awareness moment. If you and others at your company move too quickly at pushing the "aha" moment, the organization might miss the opportunity to enjoy the feelings of self-confidence, power, influence, and success. If you and others move too slowly, the organization's supreme self-confidence may seek to insulate itself further from the truth about the need for change, and it may gradually slip into the early stages of decline and disintegration.

Basic Rule 5

Effective change leaders facilitate "aha!" events to engage the organization in critical self-reflection and to catalyze a new learning path.

Change leaders must be at the vanguard to seek out opportunities to bring the truth of the surrounding environment up close and personal for the organization. They must become the canaries in the coalmine who provide early warning that mastery and self-confidence are converting to overconfidence and self-delusion. This will not be easy. Instigating or facilitating these "aha!" moments can often run against the grain of the organization's culture and challenges what, in fact, is working for most people. The first step, however, is recognizing the signs of mastery converting to self-importance and delusion. Table 1-2 highlights some common warning signs suggesting the need for change.

Table 1-2. Warning signs of decline and disintegration.

These red flags of decline and disintegration may be an early warning that the organization may need to begin a new growth curve—or suffer the consequences:

- The organization's leaders and employees often speak in terms of how much better they are than the competition or focus on the number of rewards or accolades they have received as of late.
- Dissident voices—those who challenge conventional wisdom—are ignored and marginalized.
- Creative thinkers who don't fit into the culture move to other organizations.
- People who make mistakes or experience failure are blamed and penalized.
- There is growing fatigue with pushing the envelope and increased lassitude and acceptance for the way things are.
- The revenue growth of the company is flat or declining.
- A diminishing percentage of revenue growth is generated by new products and services.
- Shareholders show decreasing interest in investing in the company.
- A culture of complacency exists.
- People are becoming risk-averse; you observe that people are less willing to venture out with new ideas.

Getting It Done

It's time to reflect upon some of the issues explored in this chapter and to apply them to your own situation. Here are two activities that will help you integrate the lessons of this chapter and begin the process of developing a thoughtful plan for successfully leading and managing change.

Exercise 1-1 asks you to identify some of the changes that your organization is experiencing today and to consider their potential implications on the organization's future.

Exercise 1-1. The changes occurring in your organization today.

Review table 1-1 for some examples of common organizational changes and then develop your own list of changes. Identify the changes that you see occurring in your organization today:

1. ______________________________
2. ______________________________
3. ______________________________
4. ______________________________
5. ______________________________
6. ______________________________
7. ______________________________
8. ______________________________

Complete exercise 1-2 by identifying where your organization is on the sigmoid curve, and listing some specific actions you can take to be a catalyst for creating an "aha!" moment (the observation point) during your organization's journey along its sigmoid curve.

Exercise 1-2. Change leader/manager actions for creating an "aha!" moment.

1. In which phase of the sigmoid curve is your organization? What evidence do you have to support this?

2. What actions can you and others in organizational leadership roles take to facilitate an "aha!" moment and help begin a new growth curve?

The results of these exercises will aid you in the next chapter in which you will focus on the key forces that are driving the changes faced by your organization.

2

Understanding the Forces for Change

What's Inside This Chapter

In this chapter you'll learn:

- The most common external forces driving change in organizations
- The most common internal forces driving change in organizations
- How these forces affect various internal organizational systems.

Why Change?

So, you think your organization needs to change? What makes you think so? Perhaps it needs to become more responsive to the marketplace. Maybe it needs to introduce a new product or service to bring in more revenue or diversify the brand. Is your organization experiencing high turnover? Is it missing its performance goals? Is there a new chief executive officer or chief operating officer on board—and what are the ground level implications of his or her vision for the future?

Every change, whether evolutionary or revolutionary, first arises in the realization that something, somewhere, needs to be, or soon will be, different. The first step for leading and managing change involves understanding the forces that are driving the change. Identifying these forces and the diverse aspects of organizational life affected by these forces is the focus of this chapter.

Basic Rule 6

The first step in leading change requires leaders to identify and understand the forces that are driving the change.

The Forces Driving Change

In his first law of motion, Sir Isaac Newton suggested that "an object at rest tends to remain at rest and an object in motion tends to continue in motion in a straight line, unless acted upon by an outside force." This principle suggests that any physical object naturally tends to resist change unless pressure is exerted upon that object by a force. If the force is great enough to disrupt the object's inertia (rest or motion), the object is nudged from its place of status quo and equilibrium to something quite different.

Although Newton's law describes the movement of physical objects in space, this principle applies equally as well to organizations. Understanding and addressing the tension between equilibrium or the status quo and the forces that are driving change in organizations are central ingredients in leading and managing change.

Chapter 1 included a description of what life would be like without change and presented the argument that change is a natural and organic process, one that is inherent with being human and of this world. Within this context, the change a person personally experiences is meaningful. It may be painful or joyful, but every meaningful personal change is anchored to a purpose: learning how to walk, leaving home, getting married, losing a job, and so forth. The importance of this concept of a purpose-driven change applies to organizations as well. For an organizational change to be meaningful, the fundamental purpose of the change must be understood by both those leading the change and those responding to it. Introducing change to an organization simply for the sake of change has few of the benefits and most of the downsides of a purpose-driven change.

The first step in defining a purpose-driven organizational change is to identify and describe the drivers—the forces that put pressure on the organization to move in a new direction. As displayed in figure 2-1, there are two broad types of forces driving change: forces that are external to the organization and those that come from within—the internal forces. Take a closer look at each of these forces and identify the specific source of energy that brings purpose to an organizational change.

Figure 2-1. Forces acting on your organization to drive change.

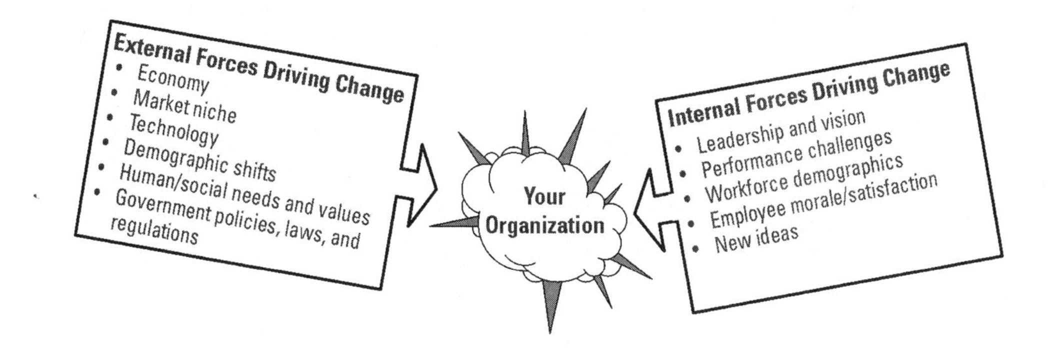

External Forces Driving Change

Every successful organization, to remain successful, pays careful attention to the factors and forces putting pressure on the organization from the outside. The most common external forces for change are described in the following sections.

Economy. The rise and fall of the economy affects the success or failure of most organizations to a significant extent. When the global, national, or local economy is booming and customers are buying, the organization might take advantage of its cash reserves or extend a line of credit to branch out in new directions, take on new customers, build new facilities, or develop new products.

In contrast, economic downturns can fundamentally alter customers' buying patterns, which, in turn, may compel the organization to pull back on its commitments, product lines, staffing levels, and capital improvements or to close some or all of its operations. As the economy worsens, banks may be less willing to underwrite expansion plans or to sustain a business struggling with cash-flow problems.

Market Niche. Every company has to continually ask itself if it is still a player in the marketplace. Changing consumer preferences, globalization, mergers and acquisitions, and vertically integrated companies that pose direct competitive threats to multiple organizations will continue to challenge the niche of every organization in the years ahead. In a world where the Internet enables almost any company to reach customers anywhere at any time—cutting across national and cultural barriers—preserving market niche is one of the greatest challenges facing today's organizations.

Technology. Technology is a principal driver for change in most organizations because it has the capacity to transform both the way work is done and nearly all of the core relationships important to the organization, such as with customers, suppliers, investors, and employees. Internet- and intranet-based communications with customers and employees, telecommuting workers, next-day delivery, and robotics in manufacturing are only a few examples of the effects of technological innovation. When applied and used effectively, technology can enable organizations to provide better, faster, and less expensive products and services, which can, in turn, increase an organization's capabilities and give it a competitive advantage in the global marketplace.

Demographic Shifts. Trends—the aging population, expanding population of ethnic minorities, growing number of speakers of English as a second language, retiring baby boomers, and an emerging Generation Next—are important drivers of organizational change. These trends, some tectonic in their size and implications, affect the kinds of products and services sought by consumers and the needs and expectations of prospective employees. Demographic changes define both the workforce of tomorrow and the consumer of tomorrow.

Companies that ignore these shifts or fail to prepare adequately for them will see their performance and profitability decline. Those who anticipate and respond to these changes will gain significant competitive advantage.

Human/Social Needs and Values. Over time, society and culture experience significant shifts in people's needs, expectations, core beliefs, and values. Individual attitudes toward work, quality, education and learning, the role of government, national identity, marriage, family, and community are all influenced by political and social events. These aggregated personal attitudes emerge as social trends that, in turn, reinforce and further shape these personal attitudes and perceptions, leading to profound shifts in the choices

Think About This

Ray Kurzweil (2001), a noted U.S. scientist, futurist, and inventor, argues that the pace of change in the modern world is moving at an astounding rate. In his famous 2001 essay entitled "The Law of Accelerating Returns," Kurzweil contends: "An analysis of the history of technology shows that technological change is exponential, contrary to the 'common-sense intuitive linear' view. So we won't experience 100 years of progress in the 21st century—it will be more like 20,000 years of progress (at today's rate). The 'returns,' such as chip speed and cost effectiveness, also increase exponentially. There's even exponential growth in the rate of exponential growth. Within a few decades, machine intelligence will surpass human intelligence, leading to The Singularity—technological change so rapid and profound it represents a rupture in the fabric of human history. The implications include the merger of biological and nonbiological intelligence, immortal software-based humans, and ultra-high levels of intelligence that expand outward in the universe at the speed of light."

If Kurzweil is right and our future will be defined by an exponential technological explosion, organizations had better start planning for the inevitable transformational change that's just around the corner—for every business in every industry.

people make as employees, consumers, and members of society. Deeply influenced by changing demographics, these shifting social needs and values have a powerful effect on what people expect from their social institutions and the businesses from which they receive products and services.

Government Policies, Laws, and Regulations. Organizations never operate outside the boundaries of governmental influence. Whether reacting or responding to or leading the preferences of consumers and employees, government always plays a role in driving organizational change. Front-page corporate scandals can lead to new laws that subsequently dictate or at least influence corporate decision making. Federal, state, and local levels of government enact laws and regulations that directly influence such issues as

- how employees are hired and how they are managed at work
- how waste from production processes is handled
- how much they are taxed

Think About This

Every year Beloit College, a small private college in Beloit, Wisconsin, publishes its Mindset List, which is a description of the world view of the incoming freshman college students. The brainchild of professor Tom McBride and public affairs director Ron Nief, the Mindset List contends that the students' world view is profoundly shaped by the events, attitudes, and experiences that define the world they were born into and that have taken place during their formative years. The Mindset List for those graduating in 2009 includes these characteristics and world-framing facts:

- Voice mail has always been available.
- They don't remember when "cut and paste" involved scissors.
- Al-Qaeda has always existed with Osama bin Laden at its head.
- Jimmy Carter has always been an elder statesman.
- Black Americans have always been known as African Americans.

The Mindset List is an eye-opening means of reminding people about the pace of change in today's world and making one mindful of others' perspectives based on their world views and when they were born.

- when and how audits are conducted
- how workers are protected
- minimum wage requirements
- how consumer information is handled (privacy issues).

Internal Forces Driving Change

The other broad category of forces driving change is that which is internal to the organization. These are the factors and forces coming from within the organization to pressure the organization, its employees, its leadership, its processes and systems, its investors, or other stakeholders (such as suppliers and employees' family members) to move in a direction different from one that they have followed in the past. Although the internal forces driving change frequently mirror what is happening on the outside (the external forces), these internal forces can also represent ideas and perspectives that are wholly independent of these external pressures. The following sections describe some of the more common internal forces driving change from within an organization.

Leadership and a Vision for the Future. Leadership, by definition, involves movement toward something and the capacity to influence others to walk (or run) toward this alternative future. The executive levels of any organization have as their primary responsibility the duty to set the direction, define the agenda, describe the desired performance outcomes for the organization, and enlist the energy of their staff toward these outcomes. Offering new ideas, challenging the status quo, establishing audacious goals, and inspiring others to bring about a shared vision are the main components of the direction setting that effective leaders bring to their work.

Performance Challenges. If the organization fails to achieve its goals in key areas such as new product development, return-on-investment, profitability, market growth, new customer acquisition, customer retention, staff retention, market penetration, and so forth, these failures put pressure on the organization to change. New goals for improving in these areas become drivers for changing the way the organization does business. There is nothing like a failure in meeting financial or quality goals or in other key areas to wake people up and drive the need for change in thinking, direction, processes, or actions.

Workforce Demographics. The workforce of today is profoundly different from the workforce of the 1960s, and it will continue to undergo significant change in the years ahead. The U.S. Bureau of Labor Statistics (http://www.bls.gov/) predicts that by 2010, 32.1 percent of the United States labor force will comprise people of color, compared with 18.2 percent in 1980. In 2000, 60.2 percent of women were active in the labor force (up from 57.5 percent in 1990 and 51.5 percent in 1980), and this percentage is expected to rise slightly to 61.2 percent by 2010. And, although these demographic shifts are really external drivers of change, they directly lead to internal drivers as organizations' workforces mirror changes in the outside world. As these demographic changes continue to unfold, the attitudes held by employees in this new diverse workforce toward work, work/life balance, job rewards, career aspirations, and other workplace issues change. Accommodating this growing diversity in employee needs, expectations, and aspirations will be a critical challenge for organizations in the years ahead.

Employee Dissatisfaction. You know that a department or work unit is having problems when turnover increases, productivity declines, sick leave rises, and overt conflicts become more frequent. These signs are evidence that something isn't right in the department and, in fact, could be terribly wrong. When employees are unhappy with some aspect of their jobs or workplace, they find ways to let you know if not directly, then through complaints and grievances or with their feet by quitting or transferring or through lower productivity. Employee dissatisfaction with organizational policies, procedures, leadership, direction, performance expectations, communication, interdepartmental cooperation, new initiatives, and the like drive change. They force organizations to make changes (sometimes reluctantly) or face the consequences: a continuing drain on organizational performance and results.

New Ideas. Finally, leaders aren't the only source of innovative ideas that challenge the organizational status quo. Great ideas—such as a compelling vision for customer service, new product innovations, improvement suggestions, and innovative strategies—can come from anyone; they should come from everyone. Healthy, vibrant organizations, especially those that are able to escape decline and disintegration, actually encourage employee-driven ideas and contributions. The challenge, of course, is that these new ideas sometimes test the status quo and attack deep-seated cultural traditions and practices that have evolved over time and that may reflect the influence of the organization's founders.

How Do These Forces Affect Your Organization?

Identifying and understanding the external and internal forces that are putting pressure on your organization are the critical first steps in putting together your strategy for leading and managing change successfully. The degree and type of change you eventually decide to initiate to respond to or anticipate these forces depends upon you and other change leaders assessing the direction and strengths of these pressures.

With a deeper knowledge of these driving forces, you can shift your attention to the targets of your change effort. The targets of a change effort are the various systems and subsystems that, taken together, define the work organization's work environment and the expectations that give focus and direction to leaders, managers, and those on the front line.

As displayed in figure 2-2, every organization can be viewed as an open system—a set of interrelated systems or components that work together to transform external

Noted

Systems thinking involves the use of various techniques to study systems of different kinds in a holistic way. It seeks to gain insights into the whole by examining and understanding the linkages, interactions, and processes between the elements that comprise the whole system. Peter Senge (1990), author of the best-selling book Fifth Discipline, *states that systems thinking is "a discipline for seeing wholes. It is a framework for seeing interrelationships rather than things, for seeing patterns of change rather than static 'snapshots.' It is a set of general principles—distilled over the course of the twentieth century, spanning fields as diverse as the physical and social sciences, engineering, and management" (p. 68).*

Seeing the "wholes" and the interconnections and interrelationships of the parts is critical to leading change effectively. Focusing your change efforts on only one organizational component, such as organizational structure or management systems, nonetheless will affect all the other components of the system. You push hard on point A and something that you did not expect happens at point F. Using a systems-thinking framework as a change leader should cause you to step back to see the interdependencies and to work through the system implications of every "small" change.

As Senge (1990) notes, "dividing an elephant in half does not produce two small elephants" (p. 66); it produces a mess!

inputs into outputs that are valued by customers, investors, and other stakeholders. These elements of each organization's infrastructure are self-reinforcing rules, tools, strategies, methods, processes, and practices that define every aspect of organizational life. They inform how decisions are made, who makes the decision, how work is performed, and who performs the work.

When there are either external or internal pressures for change, the pressure is always directed at one or more of the organizational dimensions. For this reason, this open-systems model is useful to change leaders and managers by helping them to think through and identify which of these organizational systems will be the focus of the change effort.

Let's examine these organizational systems and identify how a change might influence each.

Figure 2-2. Viewing an organization as an open system.

External Environment
Organizational Purpose (Vision, Strategy, and Goals)
External Environment
Leadership
Structure
Inputs
Organizational Culture
Outputs
Technology
Staff Behavior and Work Processes
Management Systems (Performance, Rewards, and Communication)
External Environment
External Environment
[Feedback from customers and stakeholders]

Basic Rule 7

The forces for change are always directed at one or more organizational dimensions. These are the areas of the system that are the initial target for the change effort.

Purpose

The organization's vision, strategy, and goals are directly influenced by competitive and financial pressures from the outside world (including investor concerns), by leaders within the organization who bring focus and direction in their role, by the organization's past performance, by the internal organizational capacities (for example, structure, work processes, performance management systems, technology, and culture). In any of these cases, the vision, strategy, and goals may be subject to adjustment to reflect emerging realities, diminished capacities, new leadership, employee aspirations, and so forth.

Leadership

The organization's leadership is affected by many of the same factors that influence purpose: external competitive forces and internal capacities and performance. Given these external and internal forces, leaders may need to pull back on expectations, set new performance targets, and adjust their leadership behaviors. Leaders are not just drivers of change; they must also be responders who modify their decisions and behaviors to fit changing circumstances.

Technology

Although technology is most often a driver (both internal and external) of organizational change, this component also must respond to competitive pressures, performance failures, and new work processes by integrating new tools that help translate work processes into results. As strategy or leaders demand more of existing systems, the technology system must spring into action with innovative strategies to achieve these results.

Culture

Culture is the often invisible force that works silently to influence every other organizational system. Although it is a major player in effecting change, it must also accommodate change driven from both outside and inside the organization. When a forceful, passionate leader arrives on the scene, the culture (people's beliefs, values, and assumptions) quietly adjusts to the pressure to change. When the external competition threatens the viability of the business, the culture makes room for new behaviors that, in the past, were "forbidden."

Structure

The physical architecture of an organization—its formal reporting relationships, decision-making hierarchy, functional organization of work areas, and so forth—is deeply affected by both external and internal forces for change. Becoming more centralized or decentralized, structuring around outputs and customers or structuring by departments, and reducing or increasing the levels of hierarchy are all examples of how structure adjusts to the forces of change.

Behavior and Processes

Nearly every change that washes through an organization requires changes in both leader and employee behavior. For a leader, this might involve new ways of communicating or delegating tasks that she or he might have, in the past, just done on her or his own. For employees, this might involve learning and applying a new way of performing a task, dealing more constructively with conflict, or learning how to operate a new production machine.

Management Systems

The management and control systems are created by an organization and its leaders to effectively and efficiently transform the work of the organization into useful outputs, such as products and services of value to consumers. As leaders bring new expectations, as technology creates new ways of managing workflow, as external competitive pressures put a premium on efficiencies, and when the organization experiences missed financial or quality targets, the management/control systems need to change accordingly. Such changes could include everything from developing a new incentive program to encourage team or employee performance to developing an intranet-based group scheduling/calendaring tool to aid meeting management to implementing a Six Sigma manufacturing process.

Applying the Open-Systems Model

Understanding this open-systems model for viewing an organization helps you both target your change efforts and anticipate its effects on the various organizational systems. By thinking through and identifying organizational components that need to change and discerning how they need to change, you are forming the beginnings of your change management plan.

Getting It Done

This chapter has explored the multitude of forces that may be putting pressure on your organization to move in a new direction. It also introduced an open-systems model for better understanding the interrelationships between the various systems within an organization and how these are influenced by forces outside the organization.

Complete exercise 2-1 by identifying both the external and internal forces that are driving your organization. Because every meaningful change must be anchored to a reason, it is critical for a change leader and manager to clearly identify and understand these reasons. Communicating these "whys" is fundamental to the first step of introducing change: creating a felt need or a sense of urgency (explored further in chapter 4).

Exercise 2-1. Identifying the forces for change.

Consider both the external and internal forces that are putting pressure on your organization today or are likely to in the months and years ahead. Identify at least three internal and three external forces. The more specific you are at identifying these forces, the easier you will find it to communicate these "whys" of change to others.

External Forces Driving Change in This Organization	
External Force	**Specific Nature, Quality, and Intensity of This Force**
Internal Forces Driving Change in This Organization	
Internal Force	**Specific Nature, Quality, and Intensity of This Force**

Exercise 2-2 asks you to identify the various organizational systems that are likely to be affected by these forces and, from your perspective, how they might be influenced. Developing insights into how the change is likely to influence these organizational components helps focus your change management plan and target your efforts.

Exercise 2-2. Identifying organizational systems affected by change.

Review the forces for change you identified in exercise 2-1 and each of the major organizational systems as defined in figure 2-2. Then, identify how each system or organizational component is or will soon be affected by the coming changes.

How the Coming Changes May Affect the Organization's Systems	
Organizational System	**How This System/Component May Need to Change**
Purpose	
Leadership	
Technology	
Culture	
Structure	
Behavior/Processes	
Management Systems	

With the major forces that are driving change in your organization defined, you're now ready to examine the extent to which your organization is *ready* for the coming changes. Chapter 3 presents a model for understanding and a tool for assessing how receptive your organization is likely be to change.

3

Assessing Organizational Readiness for Change

What's Inside This Chapter

In this chapter you'll learn:

- The value of reviewing an organization's past change efforts before implementing new ones
- The most common reasons why organizational change initiatives fail
- The role and importance of organizational culture in every change effort
- How to assess organizational readiness for change.

The Dismal Statistics on the Failures of Change Management

As should be clear by now, every organization, no matter how successful—and perhaps because they are successful—must embrace change as a central ingredient in its long-term success. Change must become part of the organization's culture, its way of being.

This isn't news. Most progressive, proactive organizations fully embrace the idea of embracing change. In reality, however, too few have developed the capacity or the will to introduce, lead, and manage change effectively. Here's some evidence:

- A survey conducted by Kepner-Tregoe in 1993 revealed that for 11 different types of change initiatives (including productivity improvement, quality initiatives, cultural change programs, empowerment/involvement activities, and reengineering), only 20 percent of employees indicated that these initiatives met or exceeded expectations (Spitzer, 1996).
- This same Kepner-Tregoe study found that 43 percent of nonmanagerial respondents to a survey said that their companies' downsizing and cost-reduction efforts had not met or met only slightly the objectives set. Nearly half of respondents said the same about their companies' restructuring goals (Spitzer, 1996).
- A study of 584 companies in the United States, Canada, Germany, and Japan conducted by Ernst & Young and the American Quality Foundation found that the majority of quality initiatives failed to achieve significant improvement (Spitzer, 1996).
- Michael Hammer and James Champy (1993, p. 221) estimate that "as many as 50 to 70 percent of the organizations that undertake a reengineering effort do not achieve the dramatic results they intended."
- In a study of executive perceptions by Kepner-Tregoe (1994, p. 8), nearly two out of three executives surveyed believed that employee morale was "worse" or "the same" as a result of change initiatives that were undertaken by their organizations. More than 60 percent of these executives rated their employees' reactions to organizational change as neutral, skeptical, or actively resistant.
- Kepner-Tregoe (1994, p. 16) also report that two out of three executives admitted that their organizations' internal systems (the infrastructure of their business) were "worse" or "the same" overall as a result of their change initiatives.
- A recent study by consultant and author Rick Maurer (1996, p. 56–64) found that one-half to two-thirds of all major corporate change efforts fail.

Although these statistics present a rather dismal summary of our collective track record, they do help create a compelling need for you to figure out how to do this thing called organizational change better.

Your Organization's Change Management Track Record

George Santanya, the Spanish philosopher and essayist (1863–1952), once said "Those who forget the past are doomed to repeat it." His reflections on the human condition and the path of society are especially true on matters of organizational change. Too many change initiatives fail because the change leaders fail to reflect on their organizations' history with change and on the role that culture plays in facilitating or resisting change.

Basic Rule 8

An organization's history of success or failure when it comes to change initiatives is a major determinant of its future success at implementing change.

So, before exploring a model for introducing a new change, it might be useful for you to first focus upon your organization's history of introducing change. Ask yourself these questions:

1. What has gone well with your organization's past change initiatives? What aspects of past change efforts achieved their target objectives? Which of these successful aspects could you use as a model for introducing future changes?
2. What hasn't gone well with the organization's past change initiatives? What aspects of these past change initiatives missed their target objectives? By how much did they fail to meet objectives?
3. What factors contributed to the change initiative's success or failure? What beliefs and behaviors by individuals, teams, departments, and the organization as a whole contributed to the root causes of the change effort's success or failure?
4. What are the lessons learned from your organization's past successes and failures with past change initiatives? What would you recommend that today's change leaders do differently on new change initiatives? What current practices and approaches to change would you advise them to keep doing as they approach future changes?

The results from this self-assessment of your organization's past change efforts can bring a healthy perspective to your future change initiatives. By reflecting upon the root causes of what has worked and what hasn't worked in the past, you can be prepared to do the right things and avoid the actions that can erode the success of your change efforts.

Think About This

All change efforts that fail do so for a reason. In advance of initiating a change, the most effective change leaders think through, anticipate, and prevent failure by doing the right things at all of the steps of the change process.

Before beginning a change initiative, reflect on your own organization's past success with introducing change, review the most common causes of failed change initiatives, and then develop a change strategy that reflects your best thinking on what to do (or not to do) to work toward a successful outcome and reduce your likelihood of failure.

Why Change Initiatives Fail to Achieve Their Objectives

Fortunately, you can learn what to do and what not to do by studying the experience of others. The authors' research into the factors that contribute to a change initiative's success or failure offers some useful tips for ensuring that your change initiative starts off on the right foot. The 11 most common causes of the failure of organizational change efforts are summarized in table 3-1 and described in more detail in the paragraphs that follow.

1. *Lack of urgency:* Many change efforts fail because they have failed to create a felt need or a sense of urgency throughout the organization. Before selling people on the opportunities and benefits of a change, people must first experience the need to change.
2. *Lack of a shared vision:* "Where there is no vision, the people perish" (Proverbs 29:18). Without a truly shared vision of the destination of the change, stakeholders are likely to remain in the dark as to the purpose and

Table 3-1. The most common causes behind the failure of change initiatives.

1. A lack of urgency
2. A lack of a shared vision
3. An absence of measurable outcomes
4. A failure to communicate the vision
5. Being surprised at the resistance to a change
6. A failure to integrate dissident perspectives into the change vision
7. Failing to anticipate and confront obstacles to the change
8. A failure to integrate lessons learned into the change vision
9. An ignorance of the organization's culture
10. Failing to establish interim benchmarks of success
11. A lack of structural reinforcement to sustain the change

intention of a change, making it much harder for them to bring their positive energy to help drive the change.

3. *Absence of measurable outcomes:* Closely related to the absence of a shared change vision, change efforts often fail because they neglect to define and focus on specific and measurable outcomes. Every change effort must be tied to defined, clear metrics that enable everyone from those in the boardroom to those on the front line to know if and when progress is being made on the change objectives.
4. *Failure to communicate the vision:* It's not enough to have a vision of the change and effective measures of the change outcomes. Stakeholders must understand and share this vision, they must understand the "whys" of the change, and they need to know the organizational and personal benefits resulting from a change.
5. *Being surprised at the resistance to a change:* Every change, no matter how positively it is viewed by change leaders and others throughout the organization, generates emotional stress for some. If not anticipated or understood, this emotional stress is likely to result in higher levels of change resistance.

6. *Failure to integrate dissident perspectives into the change vision:* The questions, issues, and concerns of the dissidents and other resisters who lead the push-back on the change can help improve and strengthen any change effort—but only if these dissidents are encouraged to offer their concerns. Successful change leaders pay attention to what the change nay-sayers are concerned about and then do their best to integrate these dissident perspectives into the change vision. This strengthens the change by subjecting it to rigorous scrutiny, responds directly to stakeholder concerns, and helps build stakeholder commitment to a change that is more reflective of their concerns.
7. *Failing to anticipate and confront obstacles to the change:* All organizational change initiatives experience more than a few bumps in the road. One characteristic of successful efforts is that the change leaders proactively anticipate, identify, and directly confront systemic and structural obstacles to the change vision and plan.
8. *Failure to adjust or integrate what works or doesn't into the change vision:* Successful change initiatives benefit most when change leaders have a high level of self-awareness that results from a critical assessment of the successes, missteps, and inevitable setbacks that they experience throughout the change implementation process.
9. *Ignorance of the organization's culture:* Culture (as you'll learn later in this chapter) plays a powerful and often underestimated role in the success or failure of a change initiative. Successful changes are guided by leaders who have a deep respect for and understanding of their organization's culture and its role in the change process. Because an organization's culture shapes the beliefs, values, and behaviors of people at every organizational level, it is a central contributor to the success or failure of every change.
10. *Failing to establish interim benchmarks of success:* Along with failing to define clear measures to gauge the change vision's success, the failure to establish interim benchmarks to measure the progress of the change can diminish stakeholder buy-in. Interim measures bring the added benefit of helping people see and feel progress—something that may be especially important for maintaining stakeholder motivation during a long-term change initiative.

11. *Lack of structural reinforcers to sustain the change:* In the end, one of the most significant causes leading to the failure of change initiatives is the failure to create organizational infrastructure to help stabilize the change and reinforce the new ways of thinking and acting. Without structural reinforcements, change leaders, those on the front line, and everyone in between tends to drift back into old mindsets and behaviors. As discussed in the next chapter, sustaining change commitment requires an investment in a strong infrastructure that reinforces the desired new mindsets and actions in organizational stakeholders at all levels.

Cultural Readiness and Receptivity for Change

The previous section explored some of the common reasons why change efforts fail. One of these—the failure to understand and effectively manage the organization's culture—is so critical to every organizational change effort that a bit more focus is necessary.

An organization's culture comprises a set of values, beliefs, assumptions, principles, myths, legends, and norms that define how people actually think, decide, and perform. Culture is made up of what is seen (behaviors and structures) and what is unseen (assumptions, beliefs, and values). It involves every aspect of an organization's life and the work life of everyone who is part of the organization.

Edgar Schein (2001) contends that culture is "a pattern of shared basic assumptions learned by members of a group to solve their external problems of survival in

Noted

Edgar Schein (2004, p. 32), professor emeritus at the Sloan School of Management of the Massachusetts Institute of Technology, defines culture as "...a basic set of assumptions that defines for us what we pay attention to, what things mean, how to react emotionally to what is going on, and what actions to take in various kinds of situations." Schein, an internationally respected researcher, consultant, and author, is considered the founding father of the corporate culture field of study and has been in the forefront of developing strategies for both understanding and influencing culture since the 1950s.

the environment and their internal problems of integration that work well enough to be taught to new [employees] as the correct way to perceive, think about, and feel about all aspects of their daily life." Although the external challenges for an organization relate to its financial competitiveness and its survival in the global marketplace, the internal challenges relate to issues of coordination, goal setting, performance management, collaboration, and so forth.

All these shared basic assumptions are effective when they enable an organization to stay relevant and competitive in the marketplace as well as internally cohesive and integrated to achieve the organization's desired outcomes. These cultural assumptions and beliefs are ineffective if they prevent an organization from staying externally relevant or lead to the disintegration of the internal structures that facilitate organizational wholeness and cohesiveness.

Culture, then, becomes the critical force for any organization's survival and, as a result, a key driver of or an obstacle to change. Transmitting "what works" from one person to another helps employees deal effectively with both external and internal challenges. Culture is the hidden persuader that guides and shapes employee behaviors, thereby ensuring the stability of the organization's practices and behaviors over time. Because it drives employee attitudes and behaviors and sustains the status quo, culture must be an integral part of every change initiative. If you want to lead change effectively in your organization, ignore culture at your peril.

Basic Rule 9

An understanding of an organization's culture is central to leading change successfully. Because culture influences every organizational subsystem (attitudes, behaviors, structure, strategy, management systems, and so forth), it cannot be ignored or marginalized.

Although there are no secrets or easy paths toward understanding your culture and its likely effects upon your change initiative, organizational leaders can take certain steps to predict and account for culture as they plan for change initiatives. Here are some suggestions for using your cultural knowledge to help lead successful change:

- *Know your culture.* Don't start any change without first understanding how the culture defines your organization and its relative openness to the coming change. Do an assessment of your organization's cultural strengths and potential vulnerabilities. You can go in with a vision for what you want to achieve, but if you don't know how the culture will respond you are likely to fail.

- *Understand how the culture might respond to the change vision.* With your change vision and target in mind, identify which aspects of the culture are discordant with what you want to achieve. Having a clear vision of your organization's end state after the change will be critical to your cultural change efforts. Without a clear vision, the destination is likely to be remain elusive.
- *Build your cultural knowledge into your change plan.* It's not enough to know how your culture might respond to a proposed change. You need to use specific strategies to integrate this cultural awareness into every element of your change plan.
- *Acknowledge and build on your cultural strengths.* Edgar Schein (1999, p. 189) encourages change leaders to see their culture as essentially strong and effective. If it weren't an effective culture, Schein argues, then it probably wouldn't have survived. "Always think initially," says Schein, "of the culture as your source of strength. It is the residue of your past success. Even if some elements of the culture look dysfunctional, remember that they are probably only a few among the large set of others that continue to be strengths." Schein encourages change leaders to build on existing strengths rather than simply changing "those elements that may be weaknesses."

Understanding Organizational Readiness for Change

Change readiness is the cognitive state that occurs when organizational members have positive attitudes, beliefs, and intentions toward the change (Armenakis, Harris, & Mossholder, 1993). Attaining a state of readiness is important to change leaders because those who are asked to undergo a change will be much more likely to accept the change; their resistance to the new directions and behaviors will be lower; and they will be, as a result, much more willing to embrace the change with commitment.

Change readiness is the first of the three cognitive states or conditions that people experience as they move (or don't) to embrace a change. These three cognitive states (displayed in figure 3-1) are readiness, acceptance, and integration.

Figure 3-1. The three cognitive states toward change.

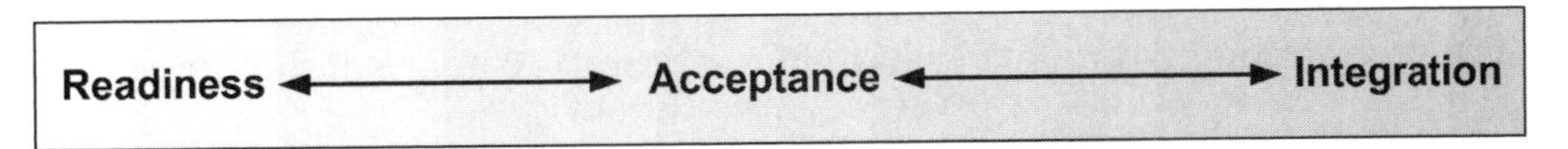

Noted

When introducing a change, change leaders should strive to develop each of these three developmental cognitive states in stakeholders as the change moves forward:

- *Readiness is being cognitively receptive to a change and is evident through a positive openness toward the change in the attitudes, beliefs, and intentions of stakeholders.*
- *Acceptance moves beyond simply being open and receptive to the change. Acceptance involves a belief in the change and a willingness to work with the change.*
- *Integration builds upon acceptance and is characterized by attitudes, beliefs, and intentions that wholly reflect the change and that are difficult to separate from the individual's routine ways of being. Integration is evident when new ways of thinking and acting (the objective of the change) are deeply ingrained within the everyday thoughts and behaviors of stakeholders.*

At the beginning of every change, those who will be affected by the change may or may not be ready for or receptive to the change. Change leaders who want a successful change outcome should first assess the level of change readiness to understand how receptive those affected by a change are now—and learn what the specific characteristics of the change or the organization are that may be eroding change readiness.

Basic Rule 10

Assessing organizational change readiness can help change leaders develop strategies for successful implementation.

It is also important to keep in mind that change readiness is a dynamic characteristic, meaning that the state of readiness shifts over time. People can also move away from a state of change readiness if the change process (or some other organizational characteristic) isn't managed well. For this reason, change leaders should continually monitor the state of readiness to determine if stakeholders are moving toward or away from readiness and if they have moved into acceptance or even integration.

The level of change readiness is critical knowledge to the change leader because eventual acceptance and integration of any change requires that stakeholders and a critical mass of individuals in the organization be cognitively ready for and receptive to the change.

Assessing Organizational Readiness for Change

Assessing organizational readiness for change involves reviewing both the cognitive state of the individual workers as well as the context and organizational environment in which the change is taking place. The major dimensions of organizational readiness and the various components within each include:

- *Organizational support:* This change readiness dimension includes such issues as the clarity of the organization's vision, the location of organizational decision making, the extent of employee participation in past organizational change efforts, the strength of the organization's training and development efforts, the extent to which employees' suggestions are listened to, the quality of organizational communications, and the extent of performance accountability throughout the organization.
- *Organizational culture:* This dimension includes such issues as the degree of cultural receptivity to new ideas or innovation, whether teamwork exists within and between work areas, the relative level of trust between leaders and employees, whether people come together when under stress or resort to conflict, the extent to which employees in the past have actively participated in change efforts, and whether people feel they are responsible for their own success in the organization.
- *The change environment:* This dimension of readiness includes such issues as the level of awareness by stakeholders throughout the organization of the forces that are driving change, the clarity of the change vision and its effects on the organization, the clarity and quality of the measures that will be used to gauge the success of the change, the organization's history with past change initiatives, the number of changes occurring at the same time, and whether the advantages from the change outweigh the disadvantages.
- *Employees' attitudes and behaviors:* This component includes such issues as whether employees feel a sense of urgency for change, the extent to which employees are fully committed to and engaged in their jobs, the degree to

which employees are able to act independently in their jobs, whether innovators and risk takers exist at all organizational levels, the extent to which employees feel that they have the opportunity to influence or affect a change, the degree to which employees are receptive to change, and whether employees have confidence in their manager's ability to guide them through the change.

Getting It Done

In this chapter you have reflected on your organization's experience with change, explored the role of culture as a facilitator or barrier to change, examined change readiness as a key factor enabling or blocking commitment to change, and reviewed the four dimensions of organizational change readiness. It's now time to integrate this new knowledge into your own practice and the change that your organization is facing.

Exercise 3-1 asks you to document your organization's experiences with introducing and leading change. This exercise will help you identify potential organizational change management assets upon which you can build and identify potential organizational liabilities. Your answers here can give you a heads-up for things to watch for as your change initiative moves forward.

Exercise 3-1. Reviewing your organization's history with change.

Reflect on your organization's experience with introducing and sustaining change initiatives. Feel free to incorporate the most common causes of failed change initiatives (table 3-1) along with your responses to the thought questions in the chapter regarding your organization's past change initiatives.

1. *Organizational Assets:* What has gone well with your organization's past change initiatives? What aspects of past change efforts achieved their target objectives? Which of these successful aspects can be used as a model for introducing future changes?

2. *Organizational Liabilities:* What hasn't gone well with the organization's past change initiatives? What aspects of these past change initiatives missed their target objectives? By how much did they fail to meet the objectives?

3. *The Sources of Success:* What factors contributed to the success of past change initiatives? What beliefs and behaviors by individuals, teams, departments, and the organization as a whole contributed to the root causes of the change efforts' success?

4. *The Sources of Failure:* What factors contributed to the failure of past change initiatives? What beliefs and behaviors by individuals, teams, departments, and the organization as a whole contributed to the root causes of the change efforts' failure?

5. *Lessons Learned:* What are the lessons learned from your organization's past successes and failures with change initiatives? What would you recommend that today's change leaders do differently with new change initiatives? What current practices and approaches to change would you advise them to keep doing as they approach future changes?

Completing exercise 3-2 will help you identify potential cultural strengths and vulnerabilities in your organization. Knowing these in advance of introducing a change will help you build your change initiative on the cultural strengths and prepare for potential cultural barriers to the change initiative's success.

Exercise 3-3 offers you a change readiness assessment tool that will give you and other change leaders insights into the relative change readiness of your organization based upon the four dimensions of readiness explored in this chapter.

Exercise 3-2. Assessing your organization's cultural strengths and liabilities.

Your organization's culture can make or break a change initiative. Although a full cultural assessment prior to introducing a change should involve conducting interviews and focus groups with key stakeholders, the questions in this exercise will at least start you thinking about ways that the culture can facilitate or disable your change initiative.

Cultural Strengths

Definition: Your organization has been successful up to the present largely because its culture has enabled high-quality results for its external customers and facilitated internal integration and cohesiveness, fostering productive working relationships among internal stakeholders.

Identify your organization's cultural strengths—the beliefs, values, assumptions, and behaviors that have enabled the organization to successfully anticipate/respond to external customer requirements and have enabled employee integration and effective team performance:

Which of these cultural strengths can be used by change leaders to help facilitate the introduction, acceptance, and integration of the change throughout the organization?

Cultural Liabilities

Definition: Some cultural elements in your organization have undercut your past change initiatives.

What deeply held leader or employee beliefs, values, assumptions, and behaviors might work to slow down or directly challenge the change initiative?

As a change leader, how will you work to prevent these cultural elements from derailing your change initiative? What actions can you and other change leaders take to modify the change or influence the culture to help facilitate the change process?

Exercise 3-3. Assessing your organization's change readiness.

Use this change readiness assessment tool to assess the relative change readiness in your organization. You are encouraged to invite other change leaders to complete this tool and then come together to discuss your collective results. After you've assessed your organization's change readiness, use the results to help you shape your change plan in a way that incorporates the readiness level of the organization.

Organizational Change Readiness Assessment

Instructions: Change leaders should complete this readiness assessment *prior* to introducing a specific change. This tool is intended as a general assessment of change readiness as *perceived by a change leader.* The level of readiness is helpful to the extent that the change leader accurately understands the strengths of these components as they may be perceived by employees at all levels of the organization. If the leader accurately senses these components *as perceived by employees,* then this tool can help the leader structure the change accordingly. If the change leader is unable to answer these questions with confidence, then the assessment will be less accurate. To increase the accuracy of this assessment, it is recommended that change leaders *gather data from others* regarding employee perceptions of these issues before completing this assessment.

Indicate your level of agreement with each statement using the following scale:

–3 = strongly disagree +1 = slightly agree
–2 = disagree +2 = agree
–1 = slightly disagree +3 = strongly agree
0 = Not Sure/Don't Know

Organizational Support Component	Level of Agreement	
1. The organization's vision is truly a shared vision in that employees at all levels understand, value, and work toward accomplishing this vision through their daily work.	______	
2. Decision making and authority are decentralized; that is, there are multiple levels of decision makers throughout the organization, and decision making isn't centralized at the top.	______	
3. Employees have, in the past, actively participated in organizational decision making, goal setting, and organizational change initiatives.	______	
4. Employees ideas and suggestions for improving their work and the organization are listened to.	______	
5. Employees view the organization's training and development programs as effective and supportive of change-driven training needs.	______	
6. The organization is effective at setting and achieving measurable performance goals and targets.	______	
7. The organization effectively uses multiple communication channels to routinely and effectively communicate with employees.	______	______ Component Total

(continued on page 44)

Exercise 3-3. Assessing your organization's change readiness (continued).

Organizational Change Readiness Assessment

Indicate your level of agreement with each statement using the following scale:

–3 = strongly disagree	+1 = slightly agree
–2 = disagree	+2 = agree
–1 = slightly disagree	+3 = strongly agree

0 = Not Sure/Don't Know

Cultural Component	**Level of Agreement**	
8. The organization's culture (its deeply held beliefs, values, and assumptions) is open and receptive to new ideas, innovation, and change.	_______	
9. Real teamwork and collaboration exist within and between organizational work units/departments.	_______	
10. There is a high level of trust between leaders and employees.	_______	
11. When the going gets tough here, people tend to stick together and help each other out.	_______	
12. Employees generally feel encouraged to innovate, offer ideas, and take risks.	_______	
13. During past change initiatives, employees have generally stepped up and actively participated in helping to shape and implement these changes.	_______	
14. People here generally feel that they are personally responsible for their own success.	_______	_______ Component Total

The Change Environment Component	**Level of Agreement**
15. People are aware of the forces driving change that exist outside the organization.	_______
16. The proposed change and its effects on all organizational dimensions (structure, strategy, processes, workflow, systems, and so on) are clearly defined and understood by those leading the change.	_______
17. When the change is completed, we'll be able to gauge our success with the change effort because there are clear measures to evaluate the change results.	_______
18. The organization has successfully implemented change initiatives in the past.	_______
19. The reason behind the coming change can be translated easily into tangible evidence that will get the attention of employees.	_______

The Change Environment Component	**Level of Agreement**	
20. The number of change initiatives currently under way feels manageable by employees who are most affected by any change.	______	
21. The perceived benefits from the change are greater than the perceived losses or disadvantages.	______	______ Component Total

Employee Attitudes and Behaviors Component	**Level of Agreement**	
22. Employees feel a sense of urgency—a felt need—for change.	______	
23. Employees have a high level of job engagement; that is, job engagement reflects employee commitment to their jobs and the company.	______	
24. Employees feel able to make decisions and act independently concerning their daily work.	______	
25. Innovators, entrepreneurs, and risk takers exist at all levels of the organization.	______	
26. Employees are generally receptive to change rather than feeling that "this too shall pass."	______	
27. When change happens, employees typically believe that they have the opportunity to influence or affect the change.	______	
28. Employees have confidence in their managers' ability to guide them successfully through the change.	______	______ Component Total

Overall Change Readiness

Readiness Component	**Scores**
Organizational Support	
Cultural	
Change Environment	
Employee Attitudes	
Total Overall Change Readiness	

Interpreting Your Change Readiness Score

If your overall readiness score is *zero* or a *negative* number, the organization is probably *not ready for the change,* and the change effort is likely to fail. Examine the lowest scoring readiness components to identify specific areas where your organization may be least ready for change.

If your overall readiness score is *between 28 and 56,* the organization has a *moderate* level of change readiness. The change effort is likely to be successful only through careful implementation and attention to the issues identified in the lower-scoring readiness components.

If your overall readiness score is *between 57 and 84,* the organization has a *high* level of change readiness. The change effort is likely to be successful as long as organizational leaders, employees, and these readiness components stay aligned with and receptive to the idea of change as the source of organizational renewal.

So far in this book, we have explored the character of change, the forces that are driving organizational change today, and the factors that influence your organization's relative readiness for change. With these chapters serving as background, it's now time to introduce the core of this book: the model for leading change and the role that leaders and managers play within this model in driving change forward.

4

A Model for Leading Change

What's Inside This Chapter

In this chapter you'll learn:

- A four-phase model for leading change
- Strategies for change leaders and managers for each phase of the leading change model
- The key challenges of each phase.

Lewin's Model for Understanding the Change Process

According to the social psychologist Kurt Lewin (1999), organizational stability is maintained when there is a balance of two sets of forces acting upon the organization. The driving forces are those forces pushing on the organization to move in a new direction. The restraining forces are those forces hindering this movement or change.

Leading change effectively, suggests Lewin, involves managing these competing forces and actively facilitating the driving forces to effect the desired change while seeking to reduce or eliminate the restraining forces. In the first phase of his three-phase change model, Lewin postulates that to introduce a change, change leaders need to unfreeze the status quo. By disrupting the organization's equilibrium (where there is a balance of driving and restraining forces), change leaders create a possibility for movement toward the change vision. After introducing the change—Lewin's second phase for leading change—Lewin suggests that change leaders turn their attention to stabilizing the gains. Lewin calls this refreezing the third phase of the change process (Lewin, 1999). His famous three-phase change model (unfreeze, change, and refreeze) is at the core of almost all models for leading change and serves as a foundation for the more fully developed four-phase model explored in this chapter.

Think About This

Kurt Lewin (1890–1947) was a German-born psychologist who, in the 1930s became one of the pioneers in the new field of social psychology. His early work in group dynamics and organization development largely defined these emerging disciplines. He wrote more than 80 articles and books.

A Four-Phase Model for Leading Change

Successfully introducing organizational change requires that leaders understand Lewin's three-phase change process and then translate these core elements into specific actions that begin with destabilizing the status quo and end with a restoration of order—but at a higher level of effectiveness. This chapter introduces a four-phase model and includes a clear, step-by-step process that guides leaders in taking the right steps to lead change successfully.

This four-phase "leading change model," displayed in figure 4-1, provides a useful framework for focusing your change leadership efforts and provides a helpful roadmap to guiding your change process.

Phase 1: Create a Felt Need for Change

The first phase of the leading change model closely parallels Lewin's unfreezing step. In this initial phase of the change process, the goal is to unfreeze the perception that the status quo is adequate to meet the challenges of the present and the future. Called "creating a felt need," the change leader's work for this stage must focus on creating a sense of urgency in the population for a need to change.

Figure 4-1. A four-phase model for leading change.

Basic Rule 11

Creating a sense of urgency—a felt need for change—is the first requirement for moving an organization in a new direction.

The goal of this phase of the change process is to disrupt the status quo such that the system being changed experiences a collapse of stable structures, thereby clearing the way for introducing a new, improved structure. The status quo could be disrupted by heightening the awareness about the need to move in a new direction. Sometimes this sense of urgency is created by revealing the peril that the organization will face if it is unable or unwilling to change. This is change driven by a fear of the negative consequences of not changing.

Table 4-1 offers a list of possible actions that change leaders can take in this stage of the leading change model.

Phase 2: Introduce the Change

Once you have people's attention, created a sense of urgency, and established the need for change, you can offer them a way out—away from the challenge or threat and toward an alternative vision of the future. In this, the second phase of the leading change model, your goal is to offer people a clear path toward a solution to the threat or challenge that you revealed to them in phase 1. Whereas in phase 1 you

Noted

Instead of relying only upon desperation and fear that the "sky is falling," change leaders can also use the aspirations or hopes of those who may need to change. By helping people envision the possibility of a better alternative future to the existence they are currently living, change leaders can tap into individual and collective hope to instill a desire to move away from the status quo and toward a better future. In either case—through desperation or aspiration or a combination of both—the goal is to shake up the equilibrium of the present, free the organization from its stabilizing structures, and prepare it for movement in a new direction. The main challenge for this phase of the process for introducing change is simply to get the organization's attention. Breaking apart status quo thinking and challenging mental models should be the primary focus of change leaders during this phase.

Table 4-1. Leader actions to create a felt need.

- Identify what needs to change.
- Determine *why* it must change and identify the problem that needs to be solved.
- Immerse employees in data from the customer, from other stakeholders, and from the organization's performance successes and failures.
- Recognize the consequences for the organization of not solving the problem or not responding to the challenge.
- Get people's attention and give them a reason to move out of comfort and complacency.

focused on selling the problem and the need to escape certain negative consequences, in phase 2 you are selling solutions—an alternative that solves the challenge facing the organization and seeks to restore a sense of opportunity and hope.

Too often, change leaders begin the change process here: They present a vision of the future to an audience that isn't quite ready for it. Without experiencing a felt need for change, few people within the organization feel a sense of urgency. Instead, they remain comfortable with the present, expressing little interest and building up

Basic Rule 12

Once people are ready for change and are out of their chairs and ready to move, the change vision offers an alternative future that provides the path to safety or to a better life.

resistance to the idea of change. Successful change leaders recognize that, without first creating a sense of urgency, those being asked to change will be much less responsive to an alternative vision of the future.

The principal challenge for phase 2 is to deal with people's fears about the coming change by channeling the anxiety that people are feeling (due to the sense of urgency you helped create) into hope and positive action. You can accomplish this in part by providing a clear and compelling vision of the future. This vision should meet the challenges of the present and future and offer specific and tangible benefits to those who are being asked to work in a different way. You can also focus people's energy on positive action by bringing to the surface their reservations, concerns, fears, and anxieties about the change and then guiding them to find answers and solutions.

The clearer your change vision is, the more able you will be to articulate the benefits of people making the change; and the more that you can listen and respond to people's issues and concerns, the less resistance you're likely to encounter in this phase. No matter how well you articulate a compelling vision and respond to people's concerns, dealing with the inevitable pushback or resistance will be an ongoing concern of this phase. You'll have a chance to explore the origins of change resistance and the strategies you can take to address these in greater detail in chapter 6. Table 4-2 presents a list of actions that change leaders can take for introducing a change and responding to employee resistance.

Phase 3: Revise and Finalize the Change Plan

As you work with introducing the change in phase 2 and begin responding to people's questions, fears, anxieties, and concerns about the change, you will soon find yourself drifting into phase 3 of the leading change model: revise and finalize the change plan. In this phase, the efforts you made in the last phase to surface and begin responding to people's concerns have begun to pay off with a higher level of employee involvement in trying to make the change work.

Table 4-2. Leader actions for introducing the change.

- Ask people to explore ideas that help solve the problem that people now realize must be solved.
- Offer possible solutions and strategies that address the challenge or problem.
- Work together with others to define the ideal state you wish to create and work together to create a shared vision of the change.
- Guide people in exploring the positive outcomes of the change and help them see the benefits and opportunities that the change presents.
- Listen to people's objections, concerns, fears, and perceived losses.
- Acknowledge their fears and what they perceive they may lose.
- Invite people to offer their own solutions to offset the perceived losses and strategies to realize the benefits; suggest your own ideas of possible gains and opportunities.
- Integrate employees' concerns about the change and their ideas for improving it into strategies that address their issues.

Basic Rule 13

Your change vision and strategy are strengthened if you integrate the insights and suggestions of those on the front line of change.

Your primary focus as a change leader in phase 3 is on integrating the ideas and suggestions of employees as they work with you to modify the change vision and strengthen the change plan. Although not everyone affected by the change will be willing or able to work with you (some will still be fighting the change), you can use their future-focused energy to begin moving forward with implementing the change.

The important challenge for phase 3 is sustaining the future-focused orientation of employees as they strive to meet the challenge of the change on their own terms. As a change leader, your primary task shifts from introducing the change to being open and receptive to constructive challenges to the change vision and strategy, making accommodations where necessary to honor employee ideas and contributions, and supporting employees as they find their own creative solutions to the challenges posed by the change.

In this phase, your change vision and strategy must itself undergo a change. What you and other change leaders first conceived as the change vision and the alternative future will need to evolve as your theories of the ideal change vision are tested by frontline realities and challenges. Change that survives phase 3 is a stronger, more effective change because it reflects real-world issues, understanding, and applications.

Table 4-3 lists actions that change leaders can take to smooth the way as they revise the change vision and strategy based on employee ideas and suggestions for strengthening the change.

Table 4-3. Leader actions for revising the change vision and strategy.

- Help people to (a) identify and explore the hidden opportunities, (b) define the future of the change on their terms and those of the organization, and (c) invent creative solutions to the challenges facing them and the organization.
- Continue to identify obstacles to change acceptance that must be overcome and explore the hidden opportunities that emerge when overcoming each obstacle.
- Encourage people to find creative answers to their questions about the change and their future role after the change is complete.
- Adjust the change vision, strategy, and plan in response to the ideas and answers offered by stakeholders.

Phase 4: Stabilize and Sustain the Change

The fourth and final phase of the process for leading change involves an integration of the hard work and the lessons learned from the previous phases and a reaffirmation of the now-modified change vision. It is a time for restoring a measure of stability to the organization by putting in place the new structures and systems that solidify the gains and reinforce the new behaviors and actions.

As B.F. Skinner's (1938) classic research into operant conditioning and behavior modification demonstrates, sustaining new employee behaviors and the behaviors of entire systems of individuals requires active reinforcement of these new behaviors. In the absence of reinforcement, new behaviors tend to be extinguished and people tend to fall back into their old behaviors. If you take away individual incentive pay as a way to reduce undesirable (non-team) behaviors, without also reinforcing the new behaviors, your employees will have a tendency to revert back to the behaviors that they demonstrated before you introduced a sense of urgency about a need for change. Even though they may have responded to the need for change and worked with you to help reinvent your organization's future, without formal organizational infrastructure that brings stability and reinforces the new behaviors, it's likely that any gains you have made will be lost.

Within the four-phase change process, operant conditioning serves as an important framework for guiding leader actions for reinforcing and sustaining desired stakeholder behaviors. Using the four types of reinforcers and punishments shown in table 4-4 can help ensure that the new behaviors will be sustained.

Table 4-4. Examples of reinforcers.

Type of Organizational Action	Example
Positive Reinforcement	• Providing a positive consequence or outcome when employees engage in the desired behaviors • Giving employees more decision-making authority over their daily work when they successfully achieve a desired goal
Negative Reinforcement	• Withdrawing a negative consequence when employees engage in the desired behaviors • Reducing managerial oversight (granting more independence and autonomy) when employees successfully achieve a desired goal
Positive Punishment	• Providing an adverse or negative consequence for failing to engage in the desired behaviors • Taking away an employee's flexible work schedule if he or she fails to achieve a desired goal
Negative Punishment	• Removing positive consequences or outcomes that, in the past, were reinforcing undesirable employee behaviors

Reinforcement is central to a successful change initiative: Change leaders must facilitate a process that builds in strong incentives and reinforcers for the new desired behaviors. As was noted in chapter 3, the failure to create this reinforcing infrastructure is a major reason why many change initiatives fail. In fact, the authors' experience suggests that too often change leaders are so fixated on just getting through the change that they significantly underinvest in the organizational infrastructure required to stabilize and reinforce the change.

Basic Rule 14

Sustaining new ways of thinking and acting by employees and other stakeholders requires active reinforcement. Without new reinforcements of the new behaviors, they will be extinguished.

The major challenge of this phase of the change process is to find strong and effective organizational systems and structures that will bring stability to the organization and reinforce new behaviors. Because there will be a tendency to fall back to known past behaviors, behavioral reinforcers must be clear, specific, and widely known. Using a blend of positive reinforcement, negative reinforcement, and, if necessary, punishment is critical to ensure that desired behaviors are sustained.

Developing an organizational infrastructure that reinforces the new desired behaviors should be your top priority for this phase. Table 4-5 lists some of the actions you can take to ensure that the gains the organization has made are stabilized and that new employee behaviors are reinforced.

Table 4-5. Leader actions to stabilize and sustain the change.

- Identify and develop action steps for stabilizing, reinforcing, and sustaining the change. These action steps might include the following:
  - — giving people time to mourn their actual losses
  - — providing skill and knowledge training
  - — revising job descriptions
  - — developing new reward systems
  - — strengthening social connections and relationships
  - — recognizing and celebrating accomplishments.
- Develop performance measures to evaluate the results from the change.
- Adjust the change vision and strategy to reflect new learning and insights.
- Challenge people to be open to new challenges, forces, and pressures for the next change.

An additional dimension of phase 4 involves laying the groundwork for the next change. Although it is important to find a new status quo in this phase, you also need to prepare employees for the next need for change. This means creating a new level of employee awareness of the environment and a new attitude toward and receptivity for the next change. Table 4-6 highlights some actions that change leaders can take to lay this important groundwork for the next change.

Table 4-6. Leader actions to lay the groundwork for the next change.

- Create ongoing mechanisms to bring the voice of the customer into the organization.
- Conduct periodic strategic-thinking sessions in departments and teams throughout the organization. These sessions should challenge people to explore data from outside the organization—emerging trends, competitive pressure, customer satisfaction data, change demographics, and so forth—and ask them to discuss potential implications for the organization today and tomorrow.
- Establish a balanced scorecard on various dimensions of the organization's performance and communicate these metrics quarterly to all departments and teams, asking them to discuss trends and implications in these critical success measures.
- Place a premium on employee-generated ideas and suggestions that reflect a strategic thinking mindset.

Getting It Done

This chapter presented a four-phase model for introducing change in your organization. It's now time for you to identify some specific steps you will take to help ensure that your change initiative is successful. Complete exercise 4-1 by listing some actions you and other change leaders will take to accomplish the objectives and overcome the main challenge for each of the four phases of change.

Exercise 4-1. Leadership actions for successfully introducing change.

For each of the four phases for introducing a change, identify specific actions to be taken by the leader and the organization to meet the objective and main challenge of the phase.

Phase of Change	Objective and Main Challenge	Leader Actions to Achieve Objectives
1. Create a Felt Need for Change	• Disrupt the status quo • Get the organization's attention	
2. Introduce the Change	• Provide a solution to the problem identified in phase 1 • Channel people's anxiety about the change toward positive action	
3. Revise and Finalize the Change Plan	• Integrate and accommodate employee suggestions for strengthening the change vision and strategy • Sustain the future-focused orientation of employees	
4. Stabilize and Sustain the Change	• Create an organizational infrastructure to stabilize the change and reinforce the new behaviors • Provide incentives and reinforcers to help sustain the new behaviors • Prepare people for *future* changes	

This chapter introduced a model for leading change that first creates a felt need for change and ends with actions for both stabilizing and reinforcing the new behaviors and preparing people for the next change. All of this changing takes an emotional toll on people, of course, and understanding the emotional fallout from change is the focus of the next chapter.

5

Understanding and Managing the Emotional Response to Change

What's Inside This Chapter

In this chapter you'll learn about:

- The emotional journey people follow during the four-phase change process
- Actions that leaders and managers should take to help guide people along the emotional journey
- The main challenges of each phase.

Charting the Human Response to Change

In chapter 4, you learned about the four-phase process that leaders should use when introducing a change. From creating a felt need for change to stabilizing the change and preparing for the next change, the four-phase model describes the steps required to initiate and sustain a change. The leader actions recommended for introducing a change, however, are, by themselves, not sufficient to help people deal with their emotional reactions.

As people move from a place of stability and certainty through the uncertainty of change and into a new way of thinking and acting, they tend to follow a predictable emotional path or journey. This journey and the actions that change leaders should take to help people along this journey are the topics covered in this chapter.

Noted

Elisabeth Kübler-Ross (1997) was the first to compare the emotional stages people experience in the face of a traumatic change to death. Her five-phase death and dying model (denial, anger, bargaining, depression, and acceptance) is often referenced by researchers and authors attempting to describe how people respond to organizational change—a type of change that is usually considerably less traumatic than death and dying.

William Bridges (1991) offers a powerful three-phase process that people experience as they move through change: endings, neutral zone, and new beginnings. His work was the first to emphasize the importance of helping people acknowledge and mourn the losses brought by a change. Bridges's work was followed by organizational consultant and author Daryl Conner (1992) who suggests that people go through an eight-phase process very similar to the famous Kübler-Ross five-phase death and dying model. Conner's model begins with stability before moving through immobilization, denial, anger, bargaining, depression, testing, and, finally, acceptance.

Daniel Oestreich (2001) offers a five-phase model in his self-published book *Our Star.* Oestreich's model begins with comfort and control before moving through shock and denial, chaos and confusion, facing a new reality, and adapting and learning.

These diverse, yet overlapping, models set out to describe the emotional path that a human being is likely to experience in the face of uncertainty and anxiety created by change. Looking across these models reveals some common patterns in the response to change, suggesting a near-universal human reaction to change. The intersections of these models indicate that the human response to change follows a predictable emotional pathway. This chapter builds upon these earlier descriptions of the emotional response to change by offering an integrative model that is deeply rooted in the four-phase leading change process introduced in chapter 4.

Basic Rule 15

The human response to change follows a predictable emotional pathway from feeling comfortable and complacent to accepting and being committed to the change.

The Integrative Model of Organizational Change

Figure 5-1 displays an integrative four-phase model. Note that the inner phases echo the phases of introducing a change from chapter 4: create a felt need, introduce the change vision and strategy, revise and finalize the change, and stabilize and sustain. This inner process describes the actions that leaders must take to introduce and sustain a successful change.

Figure 5-1. An integrative model for leading change.

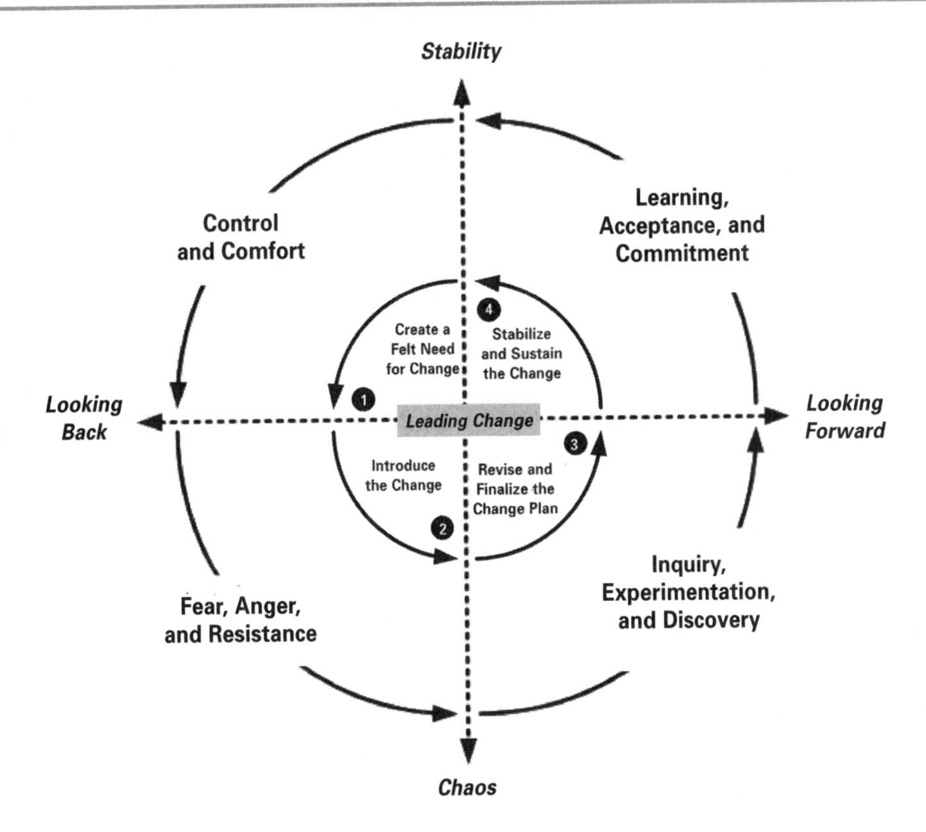

This chapter walks you through the outer ring of the integrative leading change model depicted in figure 5-1. In the descriptions of each of the four phases, you'll

- see what the change leader is attempting to accomplish (from chapter 4)
- explore the emotional state of people who are in each phase
- read about the best response that change leaders should use to both lead change and effectively respond to the emotional needs of those who are directly affected by the changes.

First, an introduction to the four-quadrant framework upon which this integrative leading change model is based: As displayed in figure 5-1, the vertical axis identifies the degree of stability and certainty within the organization; it extends from certainty and clarity (stability) at one end of the scale to the absence of certainty (chaos) at the other. The horizontal axis displays the orientation or focus of those who are experiencing the change: from a focus on the past and present at the left end of the continuum to a focus on the possibilities of the future at the right end. The four quadrants created by the intersection of these two axes capture both the level of organizational stability and the orientation or focus of those experiencing the change.

When leaders introduce change in an organization, the once-static system moves from a place of stable equilibrium and order—where everything is fixed, clearly defined, and certain—toward a place that may have considerably less certainty and, in the extreme, is characterized by disintegration and chaos. In response to the forces for change, the organization experiences a transformation in structures, rules, goals, strategies, and so forth, as it moves from stability through instability and chaos and then back to a new stable equilibrium. Throughout the change process, there is usually a significant negative effect on those who attempt to work within this churning system. Understanding and dealing with this effect—which follows a natural, inevitable, and predictable emotional journey in the face of disruptive change—is the focus of this chapter.

Beginning with the emotional phase of Comfort and Control in the upper-left quadrant and ending with Learning, Acceptance, and Commitment in the upper-right quadrant, people who are affected by a change follow a predictable emotional pathway as leaders introduce a change and as the organization moves from stability to chaos and then back to stability. Understanding people's emotional journey enables change leaders to deal effectively with the emotional reactions that they can expect to see in others when confronted by change and gives them the capacity to lead people through the change process.

Phase 1: Comfort and Control

As noted in the last chapter, to introduce a change within a stable system or organization, the change leader must first create a felt need for change. In this initial step for leading change (highlighted on the inner circle in figure 5-1), the change leader introduces a destabilizing force while confronting the emotional roadblocks to change posed by employees who feel comfortable, in control, and complacent.

The outer circle in figure 5-1 highlights the emotional phases that people experience throughout the change process. The first phase of this emotional journey is called Comfort and Control. In this quadrant of the model, people generally feel comfortable, safe, and in control of their lives. There is order and structure in their environment, giving them a sense of safety and security. From this place of stability, people understand where they fit in and what's expected of them. Even those who are dissatisfied with the status quo find a semblance of security in what they know. One characteristic of this stage of the emotional journey through change is that people attempt to hang onto the traditions and comforts of the past. This clinging or attachment to the way the world is (and, by extension, should remain) represents a major barrier to both personal and organizational growth. See the second Noble Truth in the Think About This on the next page.

Basic Rule 16

People find comfort, safety, and security in stable systems. It is this sense of comfort and complacency that change leaders seek to disrupt.

To move people from Comfort and Control toward a new direction, a change leader must create a sense of urgency about the need to change. In this quadrant, the leader's focus is on getting people's attention and moving them out of their comfort zone. The effective change leader must create conditions in which people begin paying attention to the forces that are driving change and influencing the organization and its future success. For change to take hold, people must first feel the need to move out of the Comfort and Control quadrant, give up their attachments to the status quo, and respond to the forces that seem to threaten their own long-term security, satisfaction, and health and the security of their organization.

Table 5-1 offers a list of possible actions that change leaders can take to move people out of Comfort and Control and into the next quadrant of their emotional journey through change.

Think About This

The actions of sentient beings, in Buddhist thought, are governed by what Buddhists call the Four Noble Truths (Dalai Lama XIV, 1998). These truths, first defined by Gautama Buddha (the original Buddha), are at the core of the Buddhist philosophy. The four noble truths are:

1. There is suffering, pain, and loss in the lives of all beings.
2. There is a cause of this suffering, and this cause is attachment, clinging, and desire.
3. There is a way out of suffering, which is to eliminate attachment, clinging, and desire.
4. The path to eliminate suffering involves the right view, right intention, right speech, right action, right livelihood, right effort, right mindfulness, and right concentration (called the Eightfold Path).

The attachment or clinging inherent in the second Noble Truth is relevant to leading change. The attachment that people feel to the present and the past becomes a barrier to growth and learning.

Table 5-1. Leader actions to move people out of Comfort and Control.

- Acknowledge people's successful past.
- Get people's attention! Give them a reason to pay attention so they feel a sense of urgency and understand the need for change.
- Sell the "whys" of the change. Clearly define the reasons that are driving the change forward and the consequences for the organization and for employees of not changing.
- Immerse people in specific information about the change, including customer complaints, budget data, increasing costs, competitive pressures, and so on.
- Let people know the change is going to happen—one way or another!
- Don't expect a quick response to the call for change. Give people time to let the idea and the need for change to sink in.
- Don't sell the solutions offered by the change or the idea of how the change solves the organizational challenges ahead (just yet). Instead, sell the problem that needs to be fixed and the reasons that are driving the change.

Phase 2: Fear, Anger, and Resistance

Once people understand and accept the need for change (whether begrudgingly or enthusiastically), they are soon plunged into the next emotional phase: Fear, Anger, and Resistance. This phase of the journey—marked by the absence of stable and comforting structures—causes people to feel anxious, uncertain, fearful about the future, and angry about what they are being asked to give up. These emotions surface because they have been forced to set aside what they knew to be true about the organization and their roles within it. The old dependable and reliable ways of the past and present, they have been told, are insufficient to meet the challenges of the future. The organization, as they have known it, seems less secure and more uncertain.

Change leaders should not be surprised when fear, anxiety, anger, resentment, and resistance emerge. People are anxious and upset because many of the old rules about what they have known to be true are obsolete, and they're not clear about what the new rules are or where they fit into an uncertain future. The leader's first responsibility in response to this emotional phase of change is to listen to, acknowledge, and empathize with employees' anxieties and fears. The second responsibility is to help people begin addressing their fears and anxieties about the change. This includes presenting a change vision and strategy that offer a way forward and that directly respond to the reasons why a change was necessary in the first place. By introducing new ideas, approaches, and methods that provide real solutions to pressing organizational dilemmas and challenges, the leader invites those who feel anxiety and confusion to consider an alternative future, one that with the help of their involvement and ideas holds the possibility of even greater security for the future.

Basic Rule 17

To be effective at leading change, leaders must listen to, acknowledge, and empathize with employee and other stakeholder anxieties and fears.

As part of your work guiding stakeholders through this phase of their emotional journey, you should strive to root out people's fears concerning the perceived losses resulting from the coming changes. When people believe that the change will force them to give up too much of what they value, they are likely to become fearful and angry. People feel fearful and angry about change if they think that it is the cause of their impending loss.

In phase 2, you and other change leaders should be just as concerned about people's perceptions as you are about the actual change. During a change, if people lack information, they'll make it up, and their imaginations are usually much more creative than what is actually changing! That's why, throughout a change, you must increase substantially the frequency and quality of your communications. Although effective communication should be your priority through all four phases of the change process, communication is especially important during the Fear, Anger, and Resistance phase.

To help manage people's emotional responses during this phase, you and other change leaders should bring to the surface and openly discuss the perceived losses that may be the source of people's anxieties. And, as you begin introducing new structures to replace those left behind, you should continue to stay tuned into employees' concerns, anxieties, fears, and doubts about the future and the new way of working. Your objective is either to convince people that the losses that they fear aren't likely or to offset their perceived losses with new benefits and opportunities resulting from the change.

Think About This

William Bridges (1991) writes about the endings that change often creates for people. He urges change leaders to acknowledge openly what has ended for people, what they are losing, and what they may fear. By eliciting these anxieties, the organization can face them head on, and employees can be asked to take a lead role in shaping the change strategies to help minimize these losses and fears. Once employees' fears and anxieties are reduced or offset by a perceived equivalent benefit or gain, leaders can focus more attention on the last of the emotions in this phase: resistance to new ideas.

For the change leader who clearly recognizes the need for the change, the need to move in a new direction is clear and compelling. Those who are unable or unwilling to think strategically, however, usually view the change in a very different way. Those whom we ask to accept and implement the new behaviors, methods, or processes are likely to see so-called solutions as disruptive and threatening, hence, the emergence of resistance—the reluctance or even refusal by some employees to think, work, or act in a new way.

Basic Rule 18

If you don't encounter resistance to a change, it's likely that people aren't paying attention or they're not taking you seriously.

As with the other emotional responses to change, resistance is a natural and inevitable reaction when people are asked to move in a new direction. For this reason, you shouldn't be surprised when people push back against the change. In fact, if you don't encounter some measure of resistance, it's likely that people aren't taking you or the change seriously. They may be waiting for you to move onto another big idea before they invest too much energy in fighting a change. They may be waiting for you to lose interest, shift your attention, and allow them to get back to business as usual.

Noted

The Fear, Anger, and Resistance phase of the emotional journey doesn't just create challenges for leaders and the organization, it also poses a significant challenge for people who decide to hang out in this phase. When people choose to remain in Fear, Anger, and Resistance, they assume that they are "fighting the good fight" to push back against the change while they cling to the past and present. In reality, their fight against the change often translates into eroding emotional and physical well-being.

Working against the change, hanging on to anger, dwelling on feelings of anxiety, and feeling victimized by the organization and helpless in the face of uncertainty can all contribute to this deterioration. Although it may be important and sometimes necessary to resist a change, unwillingness to face the change proactively or to try to influence the change in a positive direction often leads to a feeling of powerlessness. This sense of powerlessness, in turn, results in a self-fulfilling vicious cycle that perpetuates the feelings of fear, anger, anxiety, and helplessness.

People who decide—and it is *always* a decision—to stay in this quadrant think that they are fighting the "man," when, in reality, they are often eating away their stomach lining (growing ulcers)!

A far healthier place to be is in the next phase of Inquiry, Experimentation, and Discovery. Things are still in disarray, but one's orientation is toward the positive, proactive, and hopeful.

Resistance is part of each person's cognitive "immune system's" response to change. Everyone has an internal mechanism that evaluates a change to determine the level of perceived threat to one's identity, role, independence, and so forth. If people perceive a low threat to their sense of self from the change, they are more willing to work through their reservations and concerns and accept the change quickly. But, if the change is viewed as a significant threat to their sense of self, human beings' cognitive immune systems shift them into an adrenalin-fueled fight-or-flight response. This is true even when people initiate a positive change in their lives, such as getting married. Even when the change is of a person's own volition, he or she is likely to experience some level of internal resistance. As an example, a person may deeply believe that getting married is great, but giving up some autonomy, learning to compromise, sharing decision making, and so forth create stress and can lead to resistance, anxieties, and self-doubt.

Basic Rule 19

Involvement and participation by those directly affected by a change tends to reduce their resistance to the change while improving and strengthening the change vision and strategy.

Finally, involving others in the design of the change during this phase accomplishes two of your primary objectives: It tends to reduce employee resistance while, at the same time, it helps to refine and improve the intended change. When resisters are asked to help craft a change, they actually make the change better by bringing their practical, in-the-trenches perspectives to the proposed ideas. This increases the likelihood that the great idea proposed by you and other change leaders actually can be implemented at the front line. And, by inviting resisters with concerns and complaints to suggest changes to the change itself, the change vision and strategy are not only strengthened, but they are also left with the designers' "fingerprints," thereby reducing the intensity of people's cognitive immune responses. It is harder to reject something completely that you've had a part in developing or designing.

Table 5-2 offers a summary list of leadership strategies for managing the emotions of the Fear, Anger, and Resistance phase of the change process.

Table 5-2. Leader actions for moving people out of Fear, Anger, and Resistance.

- Provide a clear and compelling change vision that "solves" the organization's problems of the present and near future.
- As much as possible, collaborate on the vision by involving others in defining the plan for the future.
- Encourage discussion, dissent, disagreement, and debate. Keep people talking about their anxieties, fears, doubts, confusion, and hopes. Listen closely to what they have to say.
- Acknowledge people's pain, their perceived losses, and the anger they feel. Don't try to talk people out of their feelings.
- Strive to address their perceived losses by making adjustments, if you can, to the change vision and strategy.
- Communicate the offsetting benefits from the change, but don't oversell the change just to get people's agreement. Be honest about the hard work ahead.
- Tell people what you know, what's clear about the change, and what still has to be worked out. Share the questions that still need answers and invite them to help you find these answers.
- When people pose questions about the change that don't have answers, invite them to help you find answers that work.
- Discuss ways to solve the problems people see with the change.

Phase 3: Inquiry, Experimentation, and Discovery

At some point in the process of introducing a change, people's attitudes, perspectives, and orientation toward the change begin to shift. There is still considerable instability and chaos in the environment because the new systems and structures aren't yet in place. Nevertheless, if you have effectively responded to employee concerns and guided them in addressing their fears, anxieties, and questions about the change, then you will begin to see a critical mass of people whose orientation or focus shifts from looking backward to one that looks forward. When people start looking for solutions, when they seek out answers to their questions about the change, even when they begrudgingly agree to try to make the change work, they have stepped into the third quadrant of Inquiry, Experimentation, and Discovery.

You know that people have arrived in phase 3 when you see a significant reduction in open hostility to the change and a subtle increase in the number of people who are trying to make the change work. As you can see in figure 5-1, there is still a lack

Basic Rule 20

When those directly affected by a change begin searching for proactive solutions to their concerns about the change, their attitude shifts toward making the change work.

of wholeness and integration in the system, but people's attitudes have shifted to a future orientation and a willingness to make peace with the change. At this point, people begin expressing considerable optimism about the change and a strong desire for seeing the change achieve its goals. This positive energy sustains people when they encounter roadblocks and experience setbacks.

Make no mistake about it: There will be setbacks. In addition to optimism, you will also see continuing confusion, frustration, and anxiety as people struggle to find answers to some of the tough questions about the change and how to implement the new directions. In this phase of the emotional journey through change, people generally want to make the change work, but they often face significant obstacles to moving forward, among them:

- lack of a shared vision of the change
- confusion regarding the goals and objectives of the change
- questions about the change that don't have answers
- disagreements on how to proceed
- individuals brokering their own self-interested solutions
- the newness of the territory
- ongoing, low-level nay-saying from those still stuck in Fear, Anger, and Resistance
- confusion about decision-making authority.

Despite these obstacles, however, there is much that is positive in this quadrant. People's forward-looking orientation usually pulls them through the tough times toward creative strategies for translating their hopes about the change into tangible results. In this phase, people tend to be inventive and creative. They seek out positive solutions that respond to the initial challenge that the change sought to address and to their own needs, anxieties, and fears. People are asking provocative questions and, if given the opportunity, discovering answers on their own. They are trying things out, implementing things that work, and abandoning things that don't.

The organization is beginning to experience progress toward the change vision, but there is still quite a bit of work to do. This phase is called Inquiry, Experimentation, and Discovery because people are leaning forward into the change, seeking out answers, and testing strategies and solutions. As solutions are found and new systems and structures are created that reflect the change vision, the organization gradually moves back up the continuum from instability and chaos to reintegration, stability, and control.

Think About This

William Bridges (1991) calls this phase of change the neutral zone—a space that contains a mixture of both positive and negative emotions. If this conflated blend of good and bad isn't managed well, people are likely to abandon the change and slip back into the old ways of thinking and doing. In Bridges' neutral zone, people are as likely to fall backward into Fear, Anger, and Resistance as they are to move forward into the next phase of Learning, Acceptance, and Commitment. Even if people get to this forward-leaning place, there is no guarantee that they will stay there—or that they will continue to work with the change leaders to implement the change.

The challenge for leaders in this phase is to sustain the forward-looking orientation while dealing with the continuing frustrations with and anxieties about the change. People are working hard; they are tired—even exhausted—but most stay focused on the goal. If you are leading the change, your primary goal should be on keeping energy levels high and positive. How can you do this? Stay focused on the change vision while giving people the freedom and authority to find answers to the big questions about the change. Integrate lessons learned and insights from those trying to make the change work, and revise the change vision and strategy accordingly. These actions can keep people moving forward and focused on implementing the change.

Table 5-3 presents a summary of key actions and strategies for sustaining people during this challenging time and helping them move into the next phase: Learning, Acceptance, and Commitment.

Table 5-3. Leader actions for moving people through Inquiry, Experimentation, and Discovery.

- Affirm and clarify the change vision and strategy.
- Give people sufficient freedom and authority to define their own path and find their own solutions within the change vision.
- Encourage people to be creative, take risks, explore, and invent.
- Tell people what you know and what you don't know about the change. Engage them in refining what is known and in finding answers for what isn't known.
- Encourage information sharing, teamwork, and collaboration. The temptation for some people is to go off in their own direction, perhaps brokering deals and strategies that serve them personally. Encourage creativity, but try to bring people together to find answers.
- Challenge people to engage in personal reflection and learning. What can each person do to make this work? What do they need to work on to achieve this goal? How might each contribute to achieving the goal?
- Provide people the training, equipment, tools, information, and support they need to keep moving toward making the change a success. Ask people what they need to achieve a great result—and then do your best to support them.
- Revise and refine the change vision and strategy as others offer their ideas and suggestions for a successful change outcome.
- Provide people with short-term goals to ensure that they experience small victories and successes along the way.
- Be on the lookout for signs of growing frustration and anxiety. If the negatives outweigh the positives in this phase, people may lose their footing and slip back into Fear, Anger, and Resistance.

Noted

To lead change effectively, managers and supervisors must themselves be at least in the Inquiry, Experimentation, and Discovery phase of their emotional journey through change. You can't sell the need for change, for example, if you don't feel it yourself and you can't convince people to move past their anger and anxieties if you haven't moved past them yourself.

Although you still may have issues and questions about the change when you've moved into Inquiry, Experimentation, and Discovery, your orientation is toward making the change work and finding answers, rather than poking holes in the change, hoping that it will simply go away.

Phase 4: Learning, Acceptance, and Commitment

By this time in the change process, things are going well. The actions that individuals and teams have taken and continue to take are getting results. Things are falling into place. Small victories are being celebrated as the change moves forward. In this phase of the change process, perhaps for the first time, the change vision comes into a clear, high-resolution perspective.

In this fourth and final quadrant of people's emotional journey through change, individuals and the organization as a whole are seeing real progress. The new systems, structures, and processes that have evolved out of the Inquiry, Experimentation, and Discovery phase become a positive reinforcing loop: success breeds success. Synergies among people, teams, and departments emerge as new roles become defined, new relationships are built, new systems are created, and people feel more connected and integrated.

The coming together that is found in this phase results from people working hard to achieve the change goals and experiencing measurable success on these goals. These positive results and the good feelings, however, don't usually happen without a concerted effort by change leaders to help people get to this place. A big part of this success comes from the leader effectively managing both the process of introducing a change (chapter 4) and the emotional journey that people follow during change (the focus of this chapter). Guiding people from a place of Comfort and Control, through Fear, Anger, and Resistance and Inquiry, Experimentation, and Discovery and into Learning, Acceptance, and Commitment has required the leader's attention not only on the need to drive change, but also the emotional fallout from this change.

In this phase of the emotional journey through change, the leader's work shifts to affirming and celebrating the gains, guiding the building of deep organizational infrastructure to sustain the change, and preparing people for the next change. Celebrations of success help people feel that they have accomplished something important and that these gains will pay off in a stronger organization. People need to believe that their hard work has led to a positive and meaningful result. Holding a victory party is one way to acknowledge their efforts and affirm that the organization is moving in the right direction.

Building deep infrastructure that restores a new stability to the organization is a central goal of this phase. The term "infrastructure" refers to those aspects of the organization that help codify the new behaviors, roles, functions, responsibilities, actions,

Basic Rule 21

Building deep organizational infrastructure supports and sustains the change and restores a new stability to the organization.

and so forth as part of the daily workings at every level of the organization. This integration can be accomplished through a wide variety of mechanisms—all with the goal of building the new practices that emerged from Inquiry, Experimentation, and Discovery into the daily habits of the organization at every level.

Table 5-4 lists some possible approaches for strengthening organizational infrastructure in support of the change.

Table 5-4. Leader actions to sustain and reinforce the change.

Some possible methods for stabilizing and reinforcing the new ways of thinking and acting include the following:

- skill training to ensure that people have the required competencies to be successful
- establishing new performance goals
- integrating new performance standards into position descriptions and performance reviews
- providing equipment, tools, and other resources that support the new performance expectations and goals
- creating a balanced scorecard of measures that focus people's attention on a suite of key performance indicators
- establishing incentive programs that reward new behaviors by individuals and teams
- developing or refining core value statements that reflect the new directions of the organization and then using these core value statements in frequent communications to people at all levels of the organization.

Chapter 3 cited one of the most common reasons behind the failure of change initiatives: the lack of infrastructure to reinforce and sustain the new behaviors and practices that reflect the change vision. As noted in chapter 4, without reinforcers (positive and negative) and appropriate punishments (positive and negative), the new behaviors and practices are likely to wither and fade away. For these reasons, leader actions, such as those listed in table 5-4, are essential to close the loop in the emotional journey through change by strengthening employee commitment to the change vision.

Just as important to stabilizing the change by reinforcing employee behaviors in this phase, however, is the need to prepare people emotionally for the next change. The integrated model (figure 5-1) shows how stability has returned to the organization—albeit, it is hoped, at a higher plane of quality and effectiveness. This new stability then becomes the launching pad for the next need for change. Every organization, despite its desires to maintain a learning edge and engage in continuous renewal, tends to settle back into a degree of complacency and return to phase 1: Comfort and Control.

Basic Rule 22

Change leaders must balance the need for stabilizing and reinforcing the gains of change with preparing people emotionally for the next change.

Although you won't be able to stop the ever-so-subtle slide into Comfort and Control as the orientation shifts from the possibilities of the future to hanging on to what is and what was, you, as a change leader, can help prepare the way for the next change by helping to create a culture that embraces continuous change and renewal. Specific actions that you and other change leaders can take to encourage this change-oriented culture are listed in table 5-5.

The greatest challenge with managing the emotional needs of employees in this phase reflects the duality of this stage: stabilizing and reinforcing employee attitudes and behaviors while preparing them for the next change. This duality is essential for sustaining the gains from the change and for ensuring that the next change occurs with less pain and resistance than the last change. Providing stability while keeping people on the edge of their chairs requires the right amount of leadership. Table 5-6 offers some summary suggestions for leader actions.

Moving People Through the Change Journey

How long does it take for someone to travel through the four phases of this emotional journey? It depends. People tend to move at their own pace and in their own way. This journey can take 3 days or, in extreme cases, 30 years—or never!

Table 5-5. Leader actions for encouraging a change-oriented culture.

Possible methods and strategies for building, encouraging, and facilitating a change-oriented culture include the following:

- encouraging and rewarding risk taking
- providing incentives to encourage innovation
- promoting people who demonstrate the core values of risk taking, innovation, and continuous quality improvement
- exposing people at all levels of the organization to rich data about customer satisfaction and dissatisfaction, financial performance, and strategic plans
- establishing ambitious and challenging performance goals for individuals, teams, and the organization as a whole
- holding people accountable for meeting challenging performance goals
- creating cross-functional work teams to tackle substantive organizational issues by breaking down the silo walls and getting people to think outside of their departmental frame of reference
- encouraging individuals to attend professional development seminars and conferences that get them interacting and learning from their peers both inside and outside of the industry and to bring back at least one idea to change the way that they or the organization operates.

Table 5-6. Leader actions for stabilizing and reinforcing the change.

- Acknowledge what people have left behind. Recognize the sacrifices people have made. Give them time to mourn their losses.
- Acknowledge people's efforts and how their hard work has made the benefits from the change possible.
- Celebrate the successes and accomplishments of individuals, teams, departments, and the organization as a whole.
- Reaffirm the change vision as it has evolved.
- Bring people together around the vision to reinforce its importance and provide a continuing focus for future work.
- Begin developing long-term goals and plans around the new vision.
- Provide tools, training, information, and other resources to reinforce and sustain the new behaviors.
- Reinforce and reward the new behaviors through goal setting, performance management systems, and incentive programs.
- Strengthen organizational systems and infrastructure that reinforce the new behaviors.
- Build a culture oriented toward continuous learning, growth, and innovation, and prepare people for the next change.

Fortunately, as you have seen in this chapter, there is much you and the organization can do to influence the choices people make to move with or against the change. Choice is a key word here. If people move to embrace a change, if they find a way to shift their focus from hanging on to what is or was and toward what could be, that is their choice. Leaders can influence people's choices, but the choice is still theirs. If the change leaders have done their job well, more people will make the right choice to help make the change happen. Despite the best efforts of the change leader, however, there will always be some individuals who will continue to choose Fear, Anger, and Resistance as their permanent residence. Some even retreat back into Comfort and Control, withdrawing into the illusion that the organization really doesn't need to change after all.

Basic Rule 23

People always have free will when deciding how they will respond to change. Leaders can influence their choices, but, in the end, it's up to each person to decide what he or she will do when confronted with change.

Even if we get people into a positive orientation—into Inquiry, Experimentation, and Discovery—there is no guarantee that they'll stay in this future-oriented mindset. If you don't manage the confusion of this stage well, if you fail to affirm the vision, if you don't allow people to seek out and find solutions to the real questions about change, you'll see people abandoning their future orientation and slipping back into the past/present orientation characterized by Fear, Anger, and Resistance. Yes, this isn't just a one-way journey through change. The choices people make can also cause them to work against the change process.

How people, in the end, respond to the forces for change is always up to them. When you have done a good job of understanding and responding to the emotional requirements of each stage, you will see more people making choices to leave the safety of Comfort and Control, the reaction of Fear, Anger, and Resistance, the future-oriented confusion of Inquiry, Experimentation, and Discovery, and arrive with energy to spare at Learning, Acceptance, and Commitment.

Getting It Done

This chapter has covered a lot of ground! As you discovered, chapter 4 focused on the leader's role when introducing a change and chapter 5 focused on managing the responses of people through the four phases of emotional journey through change. The implication of these two chapters is that your actions as a change leader need to become a hybrid of both chapter 4 and 5 strategies. With chapter 4 behaviors, you can drive change forward and with chapter 5 behaviors you will deal with the emotional fallout that your leading change behaviors have helped instigate.

Take a few minutes to reflect upon the four-phase emotional journey through change explored in this chapter. In which of these four phases are most of your team members? Although for any given change your employees may be scattered across all four quadrants, it's likely that one quadrant is where people are bunched up. Are they stuck in Comfort and Control and unable or willing to see the need for change? Are they wallowing in Fear, Anger, and Resistance? Are they wanting to make the change work but struggling with answers in Inquiry, Experimentation, and Discovery? Or have they leaped ahead of others, landing in Learning, Acceptance, and Commitment and are integrating the change into their daily behaviors while dreaming up the next challenge or change for your team?

Complete exercise 5-1 by identifying in which of the four phases you would find most of your team, department, or work area members. What specific actions can you take to help your team members deal with their emotions in this phase and what can you do to help them move into the next phase?

Exercise 5-1. Guiding your team through its current phase of change.

1. In which emotional phase of change are most of your team, department, or work unit members?

   ☐ Comfort and Control

   ☐ Fear, Anger, and Resistance

   ☐ Inquiry, Experimentation, and Discovery

   ☐ Learning, Acceptance, and Commitment

2. What actions can you take to move your team successfully into the next phase? (Note: If your team is largely in the Learning, Acceptance, and Commitment phase, your focus should turn to how to ensure that people stay committed to the change, that your organization sustains the learning edge, and that people are prepared for the next change.)

Knowing in advance of introducing a change how you and other change leaders might help people deal with the emotions of the change journey will help you prepare for and more successfully facilitate change acceptance and commitment in your organization. Exercise 5-2 asks you to identify some possible actions that you and other change leaders can take in each of the four quadrants to help meet the emotional needs of people who are in the various emotional phases and move them into the next phase. Use the tables throughout this chapter for ideas, but, as best you can, try to customize your lists to reflect the specific change you are leading and the operational realities and culture of your organization.

Exercise 5-2. Leader actions for successfully introducing change.

Phase of the Emotional Journey Through Change	Main Challenges	Leader Actions to Deal With Emotional Needs of This Phase and Help Move People Into the Next Phase
Comfort and Control	• Create a sense of urgency about the need to change	
Fear, Anger, and Resistance	• Listen to and understand people's fears and anxieties • Present a clear vision of the change • Collaborate on the change vision	
Inquiry, Experimentation, and Discovery	• Manage the positive chaos • Sustain forward-looking orientation	
Learning, Acceptance, and Commitment	• Affirm and stabilize the gains • Build infrastructure to sustain the change • Prepare people for future changes	

In this chapter you have learned that the emotional journey people take through change follows a natural and inevitable path. You have also learned that resistance is a key factor that influences both the duration and intensity of the pushback that people are likely to exhibit in the face of most changes. In our next chapter, chapter 6, we'll explore the most common origins of resistance and offer you some tips on ways to deal with it when it inevitably surfaces.

6

Understanding and Dealing With Resistance to Change

What's Inside This Chapter

In this chapter you'll learn:

- Why people tend to resist change
- The most common perceived losses of change
- Suggested actions that change leaders can take to help reduce or eliminate the perceived losses of change
- Why change leaders should value change resisters.

The Roots of Resistance

It's a widely accepted maxim that people naturally resist change. Most change books you find—including this one—have chapters on understanding and dealing with change resistance. It makes sense. Change initiatives seem to always spawn resistance. It's hard to argue that people naturally embrace change when one observes the amount and intensity of resistance to nearly all change efforts.

This chapter begins in the same way chapter 1 did—with a contrarian's argument. Chapter 1 argued that people were naturally drawn to change, that people seek it out and embrace change as part of being alive. Consider some common life changes that most people experience during their lifetimes:

- discovering the joy of reading
- making a new friend
- learning how to talk with someone of the opposite sex
- learning how to drive a car or ride the bus or subway
- stepping out into an independent life
- tackling a new job
- getting married
- having children
- seeking out job promotions and advancements.

As you scan this list, ask yourself which of these changes you've experienced. Did you personally seek out the change? Did you welcome it? Did you embrace the change of learning how to live on your own? Or wrapping your mind around a new book? Or meeting someone new? In most cases and for most people, the answer would be a resounding "yes!" Why do people typically view these changes as those that they hunger for? Why is this list of changes different from the changes that your organization might be trying to advance?

The answer lies very much in the locus of control. Who is driving the change? Who is influencing its course? Basically, whose change is it? When people are in the driver's seat of change and charting its course, they tend to embrace the change because they desire it and are making it happen on their own terms. But, when others are doing the driving and people feel trapped, powerless, or victimized by the change (and those who are doing the driving), it makes some sense that the reaction is resistance.

Basic Rule 24

People don't resist change as much as they resist being changed! When a person is in the driver's seat of the change, he or she tends to embrace it. But, when change is something "done" to people, they tend to push back in the form of resistance.

This is an important insight for change leaders. When people are masters of their future—whether it is learning how to walk or learning a new way to interact with customers—they are far more likely to embrace a change than to resist it. For this reason, the prescription for dealing with change resistance begins with change leaders doing whatever they can to shift the driving to those who are being asked to change. This won't be easy in many cases, but it will be far easier than forcing change upon people who don't want any part of the new direction because they don't see it as being *their* direction!

Think About This

The trick with dealing with resistance is first convincing people of the need for change by shaking them out of the complacency of Comfort and Control and then inviting them to design the way out of the peril that is driving the need for change. You should still bring your change vision and strategy into view (a key step in the leading change model), just don't view your vision as the only way forward. By inviting others to sit in or near the driver's seat, you'll see lower levels of resistance and you just might end up with a new and improved change vision at the same time.

Common Reasons Why People Resist Change

Unfortunately, there will be times when you will encounter resistance. Despite your efforts to invite people to put their hands on the wheel or to help with charting the course forward, some people would much prefer just to complain about and fight the change. Many of the reasons why people would choose resistance over embracing a change involve the issue of control or influence over the change, but there are other, equally important reasons.

Ken Hultman (1998, p. 95) suggests that resistance occurs "at the moment when fear overtakes desire as our dominant motive." So, why would "fear overtake desire" when change is introduced? John Kotter and Leonard Schlesinger (1979) offer four primary factors that drive change resistance:

- fear of losing something of value (parochial self-interest)
- misunderstanding and lack of trust
- disagreements about the need for and merits of the change
- low personal tolerance for change.

Others, including Randall Dunham (1984) and Paul Strebel (1996), describe similar factors that lead to resistance to change. Effective change leaders recognize that some level of resistance goes with any change and, therefore, take proactive steps to better understand and deal with its causes early on in the process. Successful change leaders work hard at understanding the root causes of resistance and then work even harder at addressing the root causes. For some causes, such as perceived losses, the path to a resolution may be easy. For others—particularly around those related to trust and low personal tolerance for change—addressing resistance is likely to be more challenging.

Basic Rule 25

Instead of arguing with resisters, discover and directly deal with the root causes of their resistance.

Let's take a look at each one of these common sources of resistance and explore some possible leadership strategies for addressing their origins.

Fear of Losing Something of Value

Change, by its very nature, is a disruption of the status quo. If you're a change leader, that disruption is exactly what you want and what's needed for the organization to "unfreeze" and move in a new direction. If you're in the line of fire for change, that is, if the proposed change threatens to deprive you of the things that you value, then there's a good chance you will turn against the change.

The thing that people are most fearful of losing, of course, is specific to each individual. For some people, the loss of a job is devastating; for others, it would be only a temporary setback presenting an opportunity for growth. Change leaders need to spend time anticipating the range of real and perceived losses and be prepared to help people either realize that the loss is not likely or that the loss is real but will be offset by a gain.

Table 6-1 lists the 12 most common losses that some people may experience for some changes. These "some" and "may" qualifiers are important because the change may or may not lead to these losses for some of those in the path of change. Your task is to help sort out these potential losses for people and the real likelihood of those losses happening.

Table 6-1. The most common perceived losses associated with change.

Loss	Description
1. Job Security	People may fear job loss or a loss of financial resources due to a reduction in their job or income level.
2. Psychological Comfort/Security	People want to feel safe, secure, and comfortable. They may perceive that the change threatens their level of safety, comfort, security, and self-confidence by reducing their level of certainty about the world around them.
3. Control Over One's Future	Related to the perceived loss of psychological comfort and security, people may perceive that the change threatens their ability to control their future actions, decisions, and identity.
4. Purpose or Meaning	People may perceive that their fundamental purpose and meaning in life is jeopardized. Change, they believe, threatens to take away their identity, hopes, aspirations, and a meaningful life.
5. Competence	People may believe that the change will reduce their ability to do their work or jobs well. They may feel unprepared for new responsibilities and duties, possibly leading to embarrassment and a reduction in self-confidence.
6. Social Connections	People may believe that their social contacts with customers, co-workers, or managers will disappear. This can lead them to believe they've lost their sense of belonging, their role in the community, or social cohesion with a team, group, or the organization. Because so much of our sense of self evolves through our relationships with others, this perceived loss tends to be the most traumatic for people.
7. Territory	People may lose a sense of certainty about the territory or area that used to be theirs. This territory includes physical workspace, expertise, job titles, assignments, and psychological space.
8. Future Opportunities	When a change threatens anticipated rewards and opportunities, people fear they may lose a deserved reward that they have worked hard to achieve.
9. Power	Change can threaten a person's sense of power and influence in their organization and life. People may perceive that the change takes away part of what enables them to feel effective.

(continued on page 86)

Table 6-1. The most common perceived losses associated with change (continued).

Loss	Description
10. Social Status	People may perceive that the change will erode the status that they have achieved (through competence, influence, hard work, and so forth) compared to other people. What they have worked hard to accomplish may disappear.
11. Trust in Others	People may lose their trust and faith in others—especially leaders and others whom they have admired in the past—when the impending change threatens to take away other things of value.
12. Independence and Autonomy	When change is introduced, the perceived loss of competence creates a related secondary loss of independence/autonomy when people perceive that their ability to be self-directed and self-managed will be eroded.

Which of these losses is the most traumatic for people? Because each person responds differently to the perceived losses of change, it is hard to generalize and assume that the loss of job security is any more or less significant than loss of territory or competence. What is clear, however, is that any loss that is important to the person who is in the path of change and is perceived as real or as inevitable is likely to bring out resistance.

Noted

The loss of social connections during a change poses great trauma. Clinical psychologist Cynthia Scott (1995) argues that of all the losses people might experience during change, the loss of social connections is the hardest to bear. Because people's sense of self is defined through their relationships with others, when change pulls these relationships apart, the resulting stress can be hard to take. Scott's research is supported by the American Psychological Association (2004), which has stated that "caring and supportive relationships within and outside the family" can bolster a person's ability to cope with change.

A key responsibility for change leaders when seeking to deal with the perceived losses of change is to first find out what losses people perceive will occur due to the change. Once these are uncovered, you will be able to more effectively respond by helping people see that the losses (a) aren't likely to occur, (b) that they are likely to occur but the consequences for them won't be as severe as they fear, or (c) that the losses are likely to occur but that they will be offset with an even greater gain or benefit for them. When the losses are real for people, instead of convincing them not to be concerned about these losses, focus on helping them see the hidden opportunities that have opened up for them.

Think About This

The Chinese calligraphy for the word "crisis" comprises two distinct characters. As displayed in the figure below, one of these characters, the upper one, represents danger—the threat of significant loss, pain, or suffering. The second character represents hidden opportunity! Although not all Chinese linguists entirely agree with this interpretation, there is an important truth embedded in the symbolism: Too often, the hidden opportunity is only revealed or discovered when the individual or organization is confronted with the pressing danger. When people are pushed out of their comfort zones by danger, they then discover the opportunity that had been before them all the while.

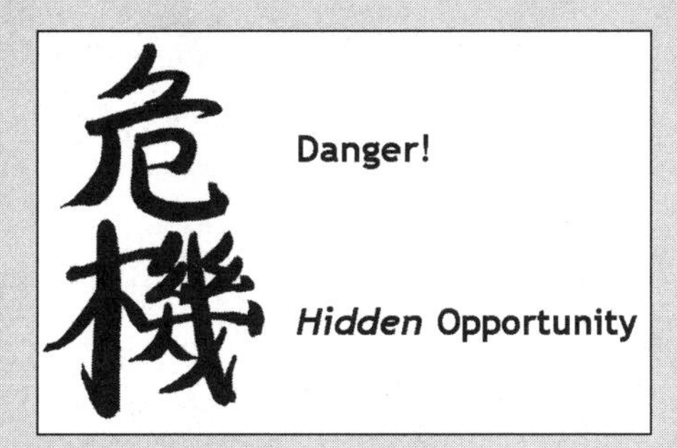

Misunderstanding and Lack of Trust

Trust lies at the foundation of so many aspects of organizational life that it should be no surprise that frequently it is at the root of resistance. If people believe that the change is designed to take advantage of them, if they don't trust the motives or agenda of those

Noted

Trust is the personal belief or faith that others, through their action or inaction, will contribute to another person's well-being and refrain from inflicting injury or damage.

who are leading the change, or if they don't believe that change leaders are acting in their best interest, then people are likely to push back against the change.

Trust typically involves

- drawing inferences about others' motives
- having predictability and consistency in the relationship
- accepting some level of risk and vulnerability
- giving the other party the benefit of the doubt in situations in where one party does not have full control.

Misunderstanding, which is more common when there is a lack of trust in the motives of the change leaders, is a significant driver of change resistance. Misunderstanding occurs most often when people don't have the information that they need to do their work and to make decisions about their future. As noted in chapters 4 and 5, you need to increase significantly the frequency and quality of communication during the implementation of change. In the absence of good information, people use their imagination to "fill in the blanks" of change, and, where there is mistrust, their imagination is likely to tend toward the dark side.

Unlike fear of loss—which can usually be responded to (but not always successfully) with reason, discussions, and offsetting benefits—trust and misunderstanding are much more difficult to address. As discussed in table 6-2, there are five kinds of trust in human relationships. Implicit, simple, and conditional trust are the types of trust that define most trust-based relationships at work. As people's trust for a leader

Basic Rule 26

In the absence of good information about a change, people will "fill in the blanks" with their imagination.

or others in an organization is tested or challenged by actions and events, these lower levels of trust can, under the right circumstances, evolve and mature into earned or authentic trust.

Authentic trust is useful in organizations because it is anchored in real experience and interactions. With authentic trust, there is a level of understanding and connection between people. This understanding and connection give people some license and freedom to take actions that affect the other party in the relationship. Authentic

Table 6-2. Types of trust in relationships.

Type of Trust	Explanation
Implicit or Basic Trust	People begin life trusting others. Vulnerable infants must rely on and trust others; this implicit trust carries people into nearly all of their adult relationships. Life experiences, of course, shape the level of this implicit trust. For example, if a person is repeatedly betrayed by trusted others, that person will become wary of trusting anyone.
Simple Trust	Simple trust is based on innocence and a need to trust others simply to survive. It is trust that has gone unchallenged and untested. Simple trust is usually taken for granted and exists unnoticed until, suddenly, it is lost. (Solomon & Flores, 2001, p. 59–63)
Blind Trust	Blind trust is based on self-denial. When people trust someone *blindly,* they see only what they need to see and refuse to look, ask questions, or truly comprehend what their eyes and ears tell them. People sometimes rely on blind trust when implicit trust fails them and they want to keep on believing everything's okay. (Solomon & Flores, 2001, p. 81)
Conditional Trust	Conditional trust is trust within specific boundaries or parameters. With conditional trust, a person trusts a party in one dimension (for example, making good business decisions) but not necessarily in another dimension (driving your project team in a car to a conference). Almost all trust is conditional. (Solomon and Flores, 2001, p. 81)
Earned or Authentic Trust	Over time, *implicit trust* relationships are tested by the events, decisions, actions, and circumstances that occur in the relationship. Over time, this implicit trust is replaced with earned or authentic trust: It is a trust that has been shaped by the dynamic interaction of two parties. It is *authentic* in that it reflects the true nature of the trust level between two parties. With authentic trust, each party now more clearly understands the trust boundaries, parameters, and limits within which he or she will operate. Each party knows how far he or she can trust the other party.

trust enables employees to have confidence in the intentions and integrity of their organizational leaders. Although they might not always understand why leaders do what they do, the employees can be confident that the leaders are acting in ways that are consistent with both the organization's and their own best interests.

When the real-world testing of authentic trust occurs, however, there are times when the threads of trust are frayed. When this happens, the level of trust can head in the opposite direction: toward its disintegration. And, once authentic trust deteriorates—because the loss of trust has evolved from real interactions and a perceived betrayal of trust—rebuilding or reclaiming it, especially during the introduction of change, is an uphill challenge. Table 6-3 offers a list of some possible actions that leaders can take to begin rebuilding authentic trust.

Disagreements on the Merits of the Change

Sometimes the fear of loss or mistrust isn't the issue. Sometimes it comes down to simply a disagreement that the proposed change is one that's worth pursuing. Kotter and Schlesinger (1979) suggest that these disagreements may be due to differing assessments as to the benefits resulting from the change and whether the proposed change is an appropriate remedy for the original problem or challenge faced by the organization.

Change leaders and organizational managers, for example, may view a proposed change as central to the organization's ability to be a successful player in an increasingly global marketplace. The pain of the change (for example, workplace disruptions brought on by broadening job responsibilities, reductions in workforce, achieving Six Sigma in production, becoming ISO 9000 certified, and so forth), from the leader's perspective, is more than offset by the fact that the company will be better able to sustain its success long into the future. Those on the front line, however, may see the disruptions as creating high levels of uncertainty and confusion without providing any guarantees that all the changes will strengthen the company. Even if the employees see that there is a need for change, they may believe that the leaders are making the wrong choices or making changes that introduce chaos but don't provide long-term security.

Because the greater the differences in these perspectives of the change or even the need for change, the greater the likely resistance to the change, it follows that you should focus on creating a shared understanding of the challenge ahead and of the change vision. Increasing your communications and interactions with those on the front line and others affected by the change is critically important for creating this shared vision.

Table 6-3. Leader actions for rebuilding authentic trust.

1. Understand Its Cause	Before you initiate a corrective action plan for rebuilding trust, make sure you understand the underlying causes of the mistrust or distrust. How did the trust first break down? When did you first realize the problem? Was the loss of trust reciprocal? Which came first? Are there multiple causes?
2. Determine the Extent of Trust Deterioration	Understanding the depth and breadth of the loss of trust will help you focus your rebuilding efforts and ensure that your response is in proportion to the problem. Going public with a mea culpa, if such is even necessary, may be the wrong action if only a few individuals are truly affected.
3. Acknowledge the Problem	Calling out the problem by acknowledging the lack of trust will get things rolling. It will also disarm people who cynically believe that nothing will change. Begin the dialog that must occur by acknowledging that there is a problem and stating that you're interested in working through the problem.
4. Start Small, but Do Something!	Take the first step, perhaps a baby step, to demonstrate your willingness to work on rebuilding the trust that once existed. The best place to begin is by simply *increasing* the quality and frequency of communications. Begin by talking about expectations, needs, frustrations, opportunities, and so forth, anything to begin building more understanding into your interactions with the other party.
5. Implement Changes	Based upon what you've heard or learned from the other party, begin to implement changes in behavior, actions, communication, methods, and so on that reflect that you have *heard* the other party and that you're prepared to do your part to improve trust. Start small and begin the rebuilding of the road one brick at a time. At the same time, give the other party the benefit of the doubt and the opportunity (and space) to take small steps in your direction.
6. Check Your Progress	How do you view the other party now? How might the other party view you and your actions? Are you both honoring your commitments to each other? Have you see a return of civility, respect, fairness, openness, reliability, and competence?
7. Don't Expect Miracles	Because authentic trust takes time and experience to develop, rebuilding it is more like restoring the vitality of an old farmstead than flipping a light switch; it is a process that may take years of hard work.

Consistent with the strategy proposed in chapter 4 as actions for creating a felt need for change (the first phase of the leading change model), bringing data-rich information into the consciousness of people at all levels of the organization can help create a deep level of awareness of why the organization needs to change. This conversation about the why of change can, if facilitated well, lead to a dialog around solutions and strategies for meeting this challenge. During this dialog, you can begin building awareness of possibilities and opportunities and looking for ways to bring together the differing perspectives on the road ahead.

The second dialog—around the change vision and the strategy about how to move forward—is your opportunity to understand the source of the differing perspectives on the change and to make adjustments to your own vision as you hear others' perspectives. Participation and involvement of potential resisters is a way to surface their differing perspectives and reservations about the change and then engage them in designing and implementing the change (Kotter & Schlesinger, 1979). Meaningful participation and involvement, if managed well, can lead to reduced resistance, greater ownership of and commitment to the change, and, most often, a better change initiative.

Low Personal Tolerance to Change

The final major source for resistance from Kotter and Schlesinger's (1979) list deals with aspects of the resister's personality, fears, and anxieties. Although most people have some short-term aversion to change—even for a positive change—some experience higher levels of these fears and anxieties. This aversion may be based in concerns as to whether they have the skills and capabilities to be effective in the new environment, but for others it may be simply anxieties with exchanging a certainty ("I know what is expected of me today") with an uncertainty ("What will be expected of me tomorrow?").

Table 6-4 lists the most common reasons why people might demonstrate resistance because of a low personal tolerance of change.

Reducing Resistance to Change

Given the variety of reasons why people might resist a change, it isn't surprising that it so easily surfaces. As a change leader, an important task you must undertake is identifying the causes of resistance and developing responses to these causes.

Noted

Edgar Schein (1999, p. 121–123) argues that, in order for change to take hold, "survival anxiety" ("If I don't change, will I survive?") must be greater than "learning anxiety" ("Do I have what it takes to make it in the future?"). For some people, their learning anxiety is strong enough that there is little room to feel anxiety about survival. For them, the in-your-face question of "Can I do this job?" takes precedence over abstract questions about whether the organization is heading in the right direction.

Table 6-4. Common causes of people's low tolerance to change.

- They believe that they do not have the knowledge, skills, or capabilities to perform in the new environment.
- Their learning anxiety is greater than their survival anxiety.
- They are trying to save face. If they were to go along with the change, it would be an admission that their previous behaviors, actions, and decisions were wrong.
- They are entrenched in and comfortable with the status quo. They believe it is better to live with the imperfect present than to face open-ended uncertainty.
- Because of peer or group pressure, they do not want to stand in support of a change when others in their circle of co-workers, friends, or family are against the change.
- Dogmatic or strong-willed individuals and those with a strong internal locus of control tend to be more resistant to change.

For each cause of resistance highlighted in this chapter, you have read some suggestions for possible leader actions. Table 6-5 offers a final integrative list that pulls together some of these suggestions and offers a few more approaches for effectively dealing with resistance.

Why Leaders Should Value Change Resisters

This chapter has focused on understanding the origins of resistance and then taking actions to reduce this resistance. Although every change leader should become a master at diagnosing and addressing resistance, leaders should also learn to celebrate what resisters bring to the change process.

Table 6-5. Leader actions for reducing resistance to change.

Strategy	Leader Actions and Rationale
Encourage Participation	If people don't resist change as much as they resist *being* changed, then one effective way to reduce resistance is to provide them an opportunity for *meaningful* participation in designing and implementing the change. Through meaningful involvement and participation in designing and implementing the change, people's resistance tends to decline, commitment tends to increase, and the change vision and strategy tend to improve.
Use Communication	During a change, if people don't have information, then their imaginations fill the gaps in their knowledge. To ensure that people are operating with accurate and useful information and that they are then able to make informed decisions about the change, change leaders need to pay particular attention to the frequency and quality of communication. Face-to-face communication is best because it supports true dialog, but all forms of communication should be used to ensure that the change message gets out frequently and clearly. Team and company meetings, newsletters, email bulletins, telephone conference calls, and brown-bag lunch discussions are all ways of getting the message out about the change vision, strategy, progress reports, milestone accomplishments, and so forth.
Organizational Support	*Training:* To address employees' anxieties about their ability to perform in the new environment (concerns about competency), ensure that your change plan anticipates the need for employee training and provides a way to deliver this training in a timely way.
	Equipment and Tools: When a change involves the integration and use of new equipment or tools (for example, machines, software, or hardware), ensure that people are trained on and have access to these tools before and as the change is introduced.
	Access to Information: Communication related to the specifics of how to perform new tasks, who to go to with questions, what the new performance expectations will be, how performance will be evaluated, and so forth helps people feel more sure and secure about what will be expected from them and who can assist them with understanding their new responsibilities.

Strategy	Leader Actions and Rationale
Provide Emotional Support	More than simply providing people the tools, equipment, information, and other resources that they need to get the job done, change leaders should also work at providing emotional support that builds self-confidence in those doing the work. Helping to create a sense of competence and efficacy in those being asked to take on new tasks and responsibilities can overcome the "learning anxiety" that Edgar Schein (1999) writes about.
Emphasize the Benefits and Provide Incentives	Help people see the hidden opportunities in the change by guiding them in exploring the benefits that will likely come their way if they embrace the change. Provide specific and valued incentives for those who adopt the new behaviors. Make sure you follow through by providing these incentives when people engage in the desired behaviors and achieve the desired goals.
Negotiate With and Co-Opt Key Resisters	Identify the leaders among those who are resisting the change and work with these leaders to understand their questions and concerns with the change. Then, based upon their issues, make adjustments in your change vision and strategy. This doesn't mean you should compromise on your core change objectives, outcomes, and strategies, but you should be able to find some areas where adjustments can and perhaps should be made. This approach demonstrates your openness to alternative viewpoints and can help turn an adversary into an ally.
Provide Negative Consequences	Although not the first strategy you will use in response to resistance, providing negative consequences to those who work against the change should be part of your mix of strategies. People need to know that you're serious about moving forward with the change. Make it clear that, with or without their cooperation, the change is going to happen but that you'd prefer it happen *with* their cooperation. In addition, indicate that their failing to help design and implement the change will strip them of the ability to make the change work for them on their terms. Your final course of action in providing negative consequences is to identify specific negative outcomes that will happen to them if they fail to adapt to the new behaviors and practices. Negative consequences, although often effective at getting immediate results (compliance), rarely engender commitment. Another downside of providing negative consequences is that it often results in unintended consequences. As you learned in chapter 1, the rule of unintended consequences indicates that you may or may not get the compliant behavior you want, but you will increase the likelihood of their resistance going underground and surfacing in counterproductive and sometimes destructive behaviors.

Yes, change resistance should not be seen as something to eliminate but as something to better understand and even celebrate. Resistance is a signal that something is amiss and that something about the change or about the organization needs to be brought to light and discussed.

According to Paul Lawrence (1969) of the Harvard Business School, "...when resistance does appear, it should not be thought of as something to be overcome" but as a "red flag—a signal that something is going wrong." He argues that when resistance occurs it's time to listen to find out exactly what the problem is. "What is needed," he contends, "is not a long harangue on the logics of the new recommendations but a careful exploration of the difficulty." Ken Hultman (1979, p. 54) offers a similar argument, suggesting that "there are times when resistance is the most effective response available" when the proposed change may actually lead to an erosion in organizational effectiveness and performance.

Basic Rule 27

Resistance should be seen as a red flag signaling that something about the change needs to be addressed.

Viewing resistance as a positive force within the change process may take some getting used to, but adopting this mindset will be critical as you work to design your change plan and build employee commitment to making the change work. Table 6-6 summarizes the major reasons why you and other change leaders should celebrate those who resist change and then work with the resisters to help move the change forward.

Getting It Done

This chapter walked you through the causes of resistance and offered insights into the actions that you and other change leaders can take to address its root causes. The chapter concluded with an argument that resistance can play an important, constructive role within the change process. It's now your turn to extract some useful insights and actions to guide your own practice.

Exercise 6-1 asks you to reflect on the potential causes of resistance to the change that you and others may be proposing for your organization or team and to list some possible actions you will take to address these causes.

Table 6-6. Why change leaders value resisters.

1. *They help define and clarify fundamental problems that must be addressed by the change.* By calling out larger or systemic interconnections and interdependencies, resisters help leaders see the larger picture that must be taken into account to achieve a successful outcome.
2. *They might identify other problems that need to be solved first.* Change leaders usually approach the change based on their own perspective on the forces and factors that are putting pressure on the organization. Resisters can help change leaders see the larger picture, which might include issues or challenges that should be addressed *before* the change is implemented.
3. *They force change leaders to think through the change before they implement it.* By asking questions about outcomes, consequences, timeline, expectations, who is affected, how they are affected, how to measure the effectiveness of the change, and so forth, change resisters force leaders to do their homework before rolling out the change.
4. *Their tough questions can improve the change vision, strategy, and plan.* By forcing leaders to think through the change (from item 3), change resisters help make the change stronger and more effective by ensuring that it passes the real-world test of those on the front line. There is often a wide gulf between the theory of a change idea and the reality of what will actually work when it hits the ground. Change resisters can improve the success of the change by making it more grounded in practical realities.
5. *They let us know who opposes the change and, therefore, whom the change leaders need to listen to.* When leaders introduce a change, they'll want to actively invite and encourage people to identify their questions and concerns. Vocal resisters may be key players who could lead others into active resistance if leaders do not pay attention to them.
6. *They slow down the change.* Because you're the one who is leading the change, you're often way out in front of those who are back in Comfort and Control or in Fear, Anger, and Resistance. Although you're ready to implement the change or even begin a conversation about the next change, others may be struggling with the need to change, or with the change vision, or with the new expectations being imposed on them. By placing a few speed bumps in your path, these resisters force you to slow down the pace of change and allow the foot-draggers and worriers to catch up to the change gradually with your help.
7. *They may be right; the change IS a dumb idea!* The tough questions, the challenging alternative view, and the contrarian perspective slowed you down enough so that you finally realized that, indeed, the change idea was a mistake. Although there still may be a need for change, the red flags of the push back raised serious questions about the change, questions serious enough to stop your moving forward with the change. When this happens, take a deep breath and say thanks to those who raised such questions about the change.

Exercise 6-1. Defining the origins of change resistance.

Reflect upon the push back on the change that you and others are introducing to your team or organization. What might explain this resistance? Review the list of common causes of resistance described in the chapter and the reasons behind these causes. Then, pull your answer together and complete this exercise.

With your potential causes identified, develop a list of possible actions and strategies for addressing these causes. Feel free to draw on ideas from table 6-5.

The Change Being Introduced:

Causes of Resistance

The likely causes of employee resistance to this change include the following:

Action Plan

The actions that I and other change leaders can take to address these causes of resistance include these:

1.

2.

3.

4.

Exercise 6-2 invites you to identify the positive contributions made by those who are actively resisting the change. Why should you say thanks to those who are working against the change?

Exercise 6-2. Valuing the contributions of change resisters.

To practice finding and extracting the value from those who offer resistance to the change you are introducing, reflect upon the push back from others and identify at least three positives from their resistance. How will you express your thanks for the value of their resistance? Describe how you will express your appreciation for the positive contributions from their resistance.

The positive contributions from those who resist this change include the following:

I will express my appreciation for the positive contributions from their resistance by:

As you have learned in this chapter, resistance is a powerful force working against a change that must be both understood and addressed directly by those leading a change. One important human characteristic that influences the degree and intensity of resistance to a given change is that of resilience—the capacity to bounce back after experiencing adversity or stress. Resilience is the focus of the next chapter.

7

Developing Employee Resilience

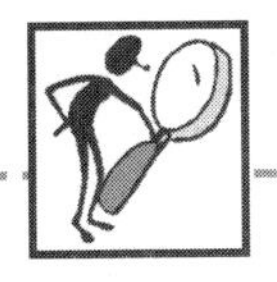

What's Inside This Chapter

In this chapter you'll learn:

- Why resilience is important to people facing significant change
- The definition of resilience and as a way of thinking about oneself and the forces driving change
- The characteristics that enable someone to be resilient
- Actions that leaders can take to help people strengthen their own resilience.

Leaders Can't Make People Change

As discussed throughout this book, an organization and its leaders can do much to facilitate the acceptance of change by people at all levels of the organization. From creating a felt need to help people move away from Comfort and Control to addressing the perceived losses of change in the Fear, Anger, and Resistance phase, to helping people explore the hidden opportunities in the Inquiry, Experimentation, and Discovery phase, to sustaining commitment to the change in Learning, Acceptance, and Commitment by creating an organizational infrastructure that stabilizes and reinforces the new behaviors, leaders play a central role in helping people come to terms with the need for change and enable them to wrap themselves around new ways of thinking and being.

Individuals themselves, however, need to make the choice to change. Although leaders can offer the invitation to change and provide a possible path to the future, whether an individual changes and whether he or she ever embraces new ways of thinking, deciding, and doing comes down to the individual choosing to stop clinging to the present and to look forward to the possibilities of the future. (See figure 5-1.) You, as a change leader, can provide incentives to help make a change more attractive to people, but, in the end, it is their willingness to, on their own, shift their focus to the future that really makes the difference.

One important personal characteristic that greatly influences the choices people make in the midst of a change is resilience. In this chapter, you will learn what resilience is, why the level of employee resilience matters, the various components of resilience, and the actions you can take as a change leader to help facilitate its development in others.

Noted

The root of the word resilience is resilire, *which in Latin means to "jump back or recoil." This root translates into the modern concept of resilience as the ability of a body to recover from or adjust to misfortune or change (*Compact Oxford English Dictionary, *1991).*

The American Psychological Association (2004, p.1) defines resilience as "the process of adapting well in the face of adversity, trauma, tragedy, threats, or even significant sources of stress"; resilience means "bouncing back" from difficult experiences. Resilience is the capability of someone to recover from and bounce back to a previous level of psychological health after being subjected to adversity or stress.

Why Resilience Matters

It is clear that the rapid pace of change in society and our workplaces has a profound effect upon those who are asked to undergo these changes. Some people seem to thrive on change. They seek out changing environments and often initiate change when things seem too stable. Others, instead of embracing a change, run as fast as they can in the opposite direction. When facing a significant change, these change-averse individuals may drag their feet, pray for a reprieve, or actively work to undercut the change initiative. Still others will put on a brave face and muddle their way through the confusion, uncertainty, and anxiety of a change. They neither embrace the change nor flee from it, but they do nothing overtly to either move the change forward or block its progress.

Chapter 6 included a discussion of how resistance plays an important role in shaping an individual's response to change. The causes of resistance, however, explain only part of why people respond the way they do to change. Resistance describes why people might push back against a change, but what explains why they might instead push forward to help drive the change? It is resilience that provides the key to explaining the positive response to change.

People who are resilient tend to face change more proactively and seek to make the change work for them on their own terms while those who lack resilience tend to endure a change, at best, and, at worst, actively avoid or resist it.

Basic Rule 28

Resilient people tend to face every change more proactively with a desire to make the change work for them on their own terms.

The Human Condition, Change, and the Role of Resilience

In chapter 6, you learned that that the feeling that a person is losing something of value is a primary driver of change resistance. The loss of psychological comfort and security is one of these critical losses. A change that leads to the loss of psychological comfort and security is particularly difficult for people to accept because it challenges the very foundations upon which their sense of self and their relationships to others are based. This critical aspect of our human condition includes several important elements summarized in table 7-1.

Table 7-1. The need for psychological comfort and security.

Stability brings people comfort.	People find security and comfort in their ability to maintain a stable order in their lives. This basic level of existence reflects a desire to achieve equilibrium and is comparable to the physiological and safety needs in Abraham Maslow's (1999) hierarchy of needs; that is, the lowest or foundational levels of his hierarchy. Satisfying basic stability and safety requirements enables a person to feel secure, in control of life, and comfortable with his or her situation.
Self-confidence and psychological health rest upon stable relationships.	With basic needs for stability and safety being met, people are then able to focus on developing self-confidence and strengthening their psychological health and integration. This is accomplished by building stable and effective relationships with others. This compares to Maslow's belonging and esteem levels in his needs hierarchy.
Psychological well-being results from environmental certainty.	Maintaining a sense of control, comfort, and psychological well-being results from the degree of certainty people have about the path or direction in their lives. When a person's actual experience matches his or her expectations about the future, the person feels a measure of control and certainty. When what is expected to happen consistently *doesn't* happen, people lose their sense of certainty, self-assurance, and, subsequently, their feelings of psychological comfort and safety.

The challenge that change presents to a person's sense of self is that it disrupts the ability to predict with certainty what's in store for tomorrow. When a change erodes people's capability to envision their own future, when it seems to jeopardize their future safety and security, or when it jeopardizes their relationships with others, they may be plunged into insecurity, self-doubt, confusion, fear, anxiety, and even depression. And, the more that a given change or set of changes disrupts this sense of self and the ability to envision the future with some degree of certainty, the greater the resulting confusion, fear, anxiety, and self-doubt.

Basic Rule 29

The more that change disrupts an individual's ability to envision his or her own future, the greater the level of confusion, fear, anxiety, and doubt in the face of change.

When people first hear of a future change, they want to see a clear picture of the change and they want to know with certainty where they fit into this future picture. Therefore, when changes are introduced—especially changes that radically alter someone's ability to envision his or her own role in the future—change leaders should help people see themselves in the future and to restore some sense of continuity and certainty. Although the new level of continuity and certainty that leaders help people create may never approximate what people once had, it at least gives them a sense of direction, focus, stability, and order.

Basic Rule 30

In the face of disruptive change, change leaders should help people see themselves in the future following a change and help them reclaim a sense of certainty, stability, and continuity.

Change leaders, however, can only do so much to help people regain their footing, re-create continuity, and restore their sense of psychological comfort and security. Fundamentally, those who are affected by a change must find their own way forward. This is where resilience comes in. When people have resilience, they are better able to find their way to a future and an optimistic orientation. Those without resilience tend to cling to the structures, ways of thinking, and ways of being of the past. They tend to be change resisters who work against the change (either overtly or covertly) and are among those who are likely to experience the most debilitating effects of a change: psychological stress, anxiety, and depression.

Effective change leaders understand the importance of employee resilience to the change effort. They know its various component characteristics and work to build and strengthen resilience in themselves and those affected by a change.

A Long History of Studying Resilience

The idea of resilience isn't new. Resilience and concepts related to resilience have appeared in literature throughout human history. The Greeks, for example, valued resilience as a practical way of understanding that life is filled with uncertainty. Poets from Rudyard Kipling to the samurai poet Mizuta Masahide to the contemporary Buddhist nun Master Cheng Yen have written about the resilient human spirit.

Modern understandings and applications of the concept of resilience to human experience date from landmark research conducted by two developmental psychologists, Emmy Werner and Ruth Smith (2001). Werner and Smith tracked the progress of 698 children from birth to beyond their 30th birthdays, seeking to identify why some children thrived while others withered when faced with significant familial and social hurdles. Their findings on resilience are echoed in comparable studies on youth under stress done by Cairns and Cairns (1995), Bernard (1991), Rutter (1977), and Garmezy (1991).

In recent years, the concept of human resilience within organizations has attracted the attention of leaders and human resource development (HRD) and organization development (OD) professionals as they have looked for ways to help employees find new sources of stability and strength in a time of great uncertainty.

Fortunately for those in search of help in understanding and developing employee resilience, the resilience of adults in work and nonwork settings has also been the focus of research. Psychologists and researchers Karen Reivich and Andrew Shatté (2003) and Robert Brooks and Sam Goldstein (2003) have examined resilience in adults dealing with stressful situations, each identifying the characteristics that enable someone to bounce back in the face of adversity and stress. Within the context of organizational change, Daryl Conner (1992) and Russell and Russell (1998, 2003) have built upon the work of Reivich and Shatté and others by inventorying characteristics of resilient people that can be used by change leaders and HRD/OD professionals to bolster employee resilience through training, mentoring, coaching, and so forth. By enhancing people's resilience, it is possible to design and implement change initiatives that maximize employee commitment.

Resilience Is a Mindset, Not a Trait

A few qualities of resilience are essential to understanding its role in organizational change efforts. These qualities include the following:

1. Resilience is a mindset and a way of thinking, not a hard-wired, innate quality. Resilience is less about who a person is and the traits he or she is born with and more about how a person thinks about self and views the world. People's mindsets directly influence how they experience threats and challenges and whether they view change as a devastating setback or as a hidden opportunity. This mindset, in turn, influences the set of behaviors people rely on in the face of a traumatic change. These behaviors can run the gamut from the classical

adrenalin-fueled fight-or-flight response, to passive acquiescence, to proactive engagement that attempts to take direct control of the change.

2. Resilience is not a static quantity. It is a dynamic quality that changes in response to the environment. A person may be resilient at certain times and not at others due to the variable quality of their own resilience capacities and the degree and intensity of the stress or change that they are facing. Because the resilient mindset is a moving target, even people who tend to be highly resilient have good days and bad days.
3. Resilience can be developed and strengthened. The American Psychological Association (2004, p. 1) says that resilience "involves behaviors, thoughts, and actions that can be learned and developed in anyone." Because resilience involves a mindset rather than genetic characteristics or even one's core personality, someone's resilience can be enhanced and strengthened. Although increasing one's resilience is always a personal choice or effort made by an individual, change leaders and HRD/OD professionals can and should facilitate its growth through effective communication, training, coaching, mentoring, and other means.
4. Resilience comprises a number of facets or dimensions that work together to enable people who have suffered a setback or trauma to regain their sense of self, purpose, and direction. By understanding and assessing the relative strength of each of these dimensions, described in a subsequent section, individuals acting alone or with the assistance of HRD/OD professionals can develop more targeted efforts to strengthen their personal resilience.

Characteristics of Resilient People

Being resilient doesn't mean that a person is immune to shock, loss, anxiety, fear, or stress. These emotional reactions are natural and expected in the face of most change. Being resilient means finding a way to keep moving forward and carrying on, usually in spite of the challenge or stress. Resilience is not being defeated by adversity but being made stronger by it.

Although Winston Churchill, Nelson Mandela, Viktor Frankl, Harriet Tubman, Rosa Parks, Aung San Suu Kyi, Anne Frank, and many other well-known world leaders and heroes offer great examples of resilience, it is important to realize that resilience is an ordinary, not extraordinary, characteristic. Resilience is something that anyone has the capacity to draw upon and demonstrate in response to adversity and stress.

Noted

During World War I, Winston Churchill served as the First Lord of the Admiralty. In this capacity, he put forward a plan to attack the Ottoman Empire, draw Bulgaria and Greece into the war on the allied side, and facilitate the collapse of the central powers. Churchill's plan was to mount a naval attack on the Gallipoli Peninsula, a perceived southern front vulnerability of the Ottoman Empire, and capture the Ottoman capital of Constantinople.

Very little went according to plan as the allied forces, entering battle with an air of invincibility, became mired in a protracted battle with the Turkish forces, who held the higher ground throughout the two-year battle. Allied forces eventually withdrew their troops, but not before thousands were killed and wounded. During the failed attempt, an estimated 131,000 solders were killed and another 262,000 wounded on both sides of the battle.

Winston Churchill and the First Sea Lord John Fisher both resigned their posts after the troop withdrawal, amid mutual recriminations as to the cause of the humiliating defeat for the allied powers. Instead of being personally destroyed by the disastrous Gallipoli campaign, however, Churchill walked away from the humiliation with a more realistic sense of British military capabilities and a resolve to never again make the mistakes that led to such massive loss of life. He subsequently drew upon the lessons learned from his earlier mistakes to lead Britain and the allied powers throughout World War II (Manchester, 1983, p. 556–563).

Think About This

"Success is not final. Failure is not fatal. It is the courage to continue that makes the difference."

—Winston Churchill

The authors' research and experience has led them to identify eight dimensions or facets of resilience. These facets have evolved from their extensive practice in leading organizations and individuals through change and are reinforced by the research of others, most specifically Conner (1992), Reivich and Shatté (2003), and the American Psychological Association (2004). The dimensions of personal resilience are described in table 7-2.

Table 7-2. The eight facets of personal resilience.

Facet	Description
1. Self-Assurance	This dimension involves individuals having a high degree of self-confidence and a strong belief that they can meet any challenge with hope and realistic optimism. For instance, self-assurance includes the understanding that, while the world is complex and challenging, a person has the ability to find the opportunities that are always present in every situation and to succeed despite the challenges of today and tomorrow.
2. Personal Meaning and Vision	Resilient people know what they believe in and have a clear idea of what they want to accomplish or create in their life. With a larger meaning and life purpose pulling them forward, resilient people approach adversity and stress with a sense of opportunity and hope. Spirituality and faith are two common elements of this facet of resilience. For instance, people's resilience helps them take a longer view of their lives; it helps them see where they fit into the bigger picture; and it provides a place for focus and clarity when they have to make tough decisions.
3. Flexible and Adaptable	The most resilient people are those who are keenly aware of and sensitive to the changes occurring in the world around them. With the help of this awareness, they are able to shift gears and direction as necessary to accommodate new realities while remaining true to their life purpose or vision. Resilient people adapt to the environment as both a survival mechanism and a vehicle that enables them to continue the pursuit of their personal goals. When people's progress is frustrated, when they reach a dead end, and when every effort they make leads to failure, they draw upon their flexibility and adaptability to make sensible adjustments to their plans to keep moving forward. Instead of being defeated, they regroup, rethink, and redefine their next steps. Mistakes and failures become lessons of what not to do next time.
4. Organized	In the face of chaos and uncertainty, resilient people find ways to create a level of order and structure that provides them the focus and stability that they need to achieve their goals. Being organized involves using a variety of simple and personalized tools that bring the structure and focus that are required for that moment. On a personal level, this facet of resilience might involve narrowing goals; breaking complex tasks into shorter-term, more achievable goals; thinking through what needs to be done before taking action; putting together to-do lists and check sheets; using a computer- or Web-based scheduler to manage time; and so forth.

(continued on page 110)

Table 7-2. The eight facets of personal resilience (continued).

Facet	Description
5. Problem Solver	Resilient people have the ability to analyze and break apart complex problems, discover the root causes of these problems, and then create lasting solutions. They are effective at seeing the relationship of a problem to other problems within a larger system or network of deeply interdependent issues. This awareness of the bigger picture enables them to recognize the limits of their own influence and to expect (and not be blindsided by) the unexpected. A person who is resilient feels able to tackle almost any problem by clearly defining and perhaps narrowing the problem, identifying its relationship to other issues and problems, and setting reasonable goals about what can realistically be expected as a result.
6. Interpersonal Competence	A key dimension of resilience is an individual's ability to understand and empathize with others. Resilient people demonstrate the competencies of emotional intelligence: a high level of self and social awareness and the ability to use this awareness to effectively manage themselves and their relationships with others. For more information on this important facet, see any of the work on emotional intelligence by Daniel Goleman, particularly *Primal Leadership* (2002). People's awareness of their own emotional vulnerabilities and capabilities helps them manage their behaviors and interactions with others to maximize their effectiveness. Awareness of *others'* emotional needs and complexities helps a person develop empathy and understanding for others. Strength in this facet enables one to maintain effective relationships even during times of great stress.
7. Socially Connected	Closely related to interpersonal competence, this resilience dimension involves the quality of a person's interpersonal and professional network of relationships. According to the American Psychological Association (2004, p. 2), the most important factor in resilience is having "caring and supportive relationships within and outside the family." Relationships that "create love and trust, provide role models, and offer encouragement and reassurance" help bolster a person's resilience." Resilient people tend to have a strong relationship network within which they share ideas, problems, solutions, frustrations, hopes, and so forth. In the face of adversity and stress, resilient people call upon this network for support, affirmation, and problem solving. The resilience facets of self-assurance, meaning/personal vision, proactivity, and problem solving are all enhanced and strengthened by social networks. This network affirms a person's capabilities while helping him or her see alternatives, personal vulnerabilities, and new opportunities that might otherwise be missed.

Table 7-2. The eight facets of personal resilience (continued).

Facet	Description
8. Proactive	Resilient people are proactive when it comes to change. Rather than simply reacting to a change, they actively engage it and, in the process, seek to shape it to their own vision of the future as they wish it to be. Proactive people tend to have an internal locus of control (Rotter, 1966) where they believe that they have the capacity and the *responsibility* to determine their own destiny vs. feeling powerless in a given situation. Consequently, resilient people tend to focus on *expanding* their influence over a change through assertive behaviors and actions. This proactive nature enables them to preserve their self-efficacy in the face of any change—even a traumatic one. Viktor Frankl's story (1997) offers a moving testament of life in the Auschwitz, Dachau, and Turkheim Nazi concentration camps. Despite being sick with typhoid and being subjected to torture and starvation, Frankl and other survivors of the camps managed to hold onto their humanity and compassion. Frankl's inspiring story about the resilience of the human spirit speaks to the power of being proactive in the face of horrific adversity. Combined with strong self-confidence and self-assurance, proactivity gives us the ability to take any situation and find a positive outcome. Although it is not always easy to find the silver lining, resilient people never lose sight of the choices that they are making that influence their response to the challenge.

In his book *Man's Search for Meaning,* Viktor Frankl (1997, p. 86) writes about seeing men walking through the prison huts in a Nazi concentration camp, comforting others, and giving away their last piece of bread. "They may have been small in number," he wrote, "but they offer sufficient proof that everything can be taken from a man but one thing: the last of the human freedoms—to choose one's attitude in any given set of circumstances, to choose one's own way." Frankl argued that, in nearly all circumstances, people always have choices: "Every day, every hour, offered the opportunity to make a decision," he goes on to say, "a decision which determined whether you would or would not submit to the powers which threatened to rob you of your very self, your inner freedom."

Nelson Mandela, another remarkably resilient individual, spent 27 years behind bars in apartheid South Africa. In his 1994 autobiography, *Long Walk to Freedom* (p. 552–558), Mandela noted that, upon entering the infamous Robben Island prison, he vowed to maintain his dignity despite the efforts of the prison and the authorities to take it away. "For any man or institution," he writes, "that tries to rob me of my dignity will lose because I will not part with it at any price or under any pressure." From his tiny prison cell, he successfully negotiated the peaceful transition to a post-apartheid South Africa, where he became its first democratically elected president.

Noted

Emotional intelligence has emerged in recent years as an important contribution to the literature on personal effectiveness and leadership. Popularized by Howard Gardner, Wayne Payne, and most recently Daniel Goleman, emotional intelligence contains some important truths and insights for those who lead change. Goleman (2004) identifies the five competencies of emotional intelligence as

- *a person's ability to identify his or her emotional states and to understand the internal linkages between emotions, thoughts, and actions*
- *the capacity to manage your own emotional states by controlling your emotions or shifting from undesirable emotional states to more productive ones*
- *the ability to freely enter into emotional states that are associated with a drive to achieve and be successful*
- *the capacity to read, be sensitive, and influence other people's emotions*
- *the ability to enter and sustain satisfactory interpersonal relationships.*

Change leaders who are emotionally intelligent—with strengths in all of these five competencies—will have a greater ability to guide others along the emotional journey of change. By being aware of the emotional requirements and needs of others, change leaders will be more able to respond with empathy and understanding. With greater awareness and control over their own emotions, change leaders will be much more able to act appropriately in stressful situations—and there will be a few!

Assessing Resilience

Resilience is a dynamic characteristic; that is, it changes over time. There are some periods of life in which we are very resilient and able to withstand almost any adversity. There are other times in our life when even small setbacks or bumps in the road can cause people to lose their balance and feel defeated or feel that they don't have what it takes.

It's important to recognize the variable nature of resilience and to use this insight to continue working at building and strengthening aspects of resilience. Taking stock of your own resilience levels in each of the eight resilience dimensions can help you focus on areas where you can become stronger and more resilient. You can also, in your role as a change leader, help others assess and strengthen their resilience.

Table 7-3 lists a series of statements that seek to measure the level of resilience for each of the eight resilience facets. This list is taken from a longer inventory that measures resilience called the resilience quotient or RQ. The complete RQ tool is available from the authors.

Developing Resilience in Others

Because each person has different resilience capacities, strengths, and vulnerabilities, developing resilience requires an individualized approach. In addition, people react differently to stress and trauma. Faced with the same challenge—for example, the introduction of new performance standards and more accurate measures of accountability—some employees would view the change as a challenge to be met while others would react with anxiety and fear and may choose this as an opportunity to quit their job.

Basic Rule 31

Facing the same change, some people react with anxiety, fear, anger, and even depression while others view the change as filled with opportunity and promise.

Furthermore, what works at strengthening resilience in some people, such as sending them to a classroom training session to learn a new required skill, won't work for others who might, for example, benefit more from one-on-one coaching. Cultural and ethnic differences may play an important role in influencing resilience, and change leaders should be particularly aware of these factors when creating individual resilience development plans.

Table 7-4 presents a summary of the actions that individuals can take to build their own resilience.

Table 7-3. Measuring resilience.

The following statements, taken from a longer resilience quotient tool developed by the authors, should all be answered using a six-point scale: 1 = strongly disagree, 2 = disagree, 3 = slightly disagree, 4 = slightly agree, 5 = agree, 6 = strongly agree.

Resilience Facet	Sample Measurement Statements	Rating 1	2	3	4	5	6
1. Self-Assurance	• I believe that I have the knowledge, skills, and abilities to deal with almost anything that happens to me.	☐	☐	☐	☐	☐	☐
	• I think and speak positively about myself and my abilities when facing a challenge or stress.	☐	☐	☐	☐	☐	☐
2. Personal Meaning and Vision	• I know what's important to me in my life.	☐	☐	☐	☐	☐	☐
	• When I look back on my life, I see a clear pattern in the choices and decisions that I have made.	☐	☐	☐	☐	☐	☐
3. Flexible and Adaptable	• I approach new situations with an open mind as to what needs to be done.	☐	☐	☐	☐	☐	☐
	• I am willing and able to make adjustments to my goals and plans when situations and expectations of me change.	☐	☐	☐	☐	☐	☐
4. Organized	• When faced with a major change, I usually find a way to create systems or structures that give me a degree of control that I find useful and helpful.	☐	☐	☐	☐	☐	☐
	• I start each workday by thinking about what I need to accomplish during that day and I end each day reviewing what I need to accomplish the next day.	☐	☐	☐	☐	☐	☐
5. Problem Solver	• When I have a problem to solve or a decision to make, I usually spend time defining the problem or decision.	☐	☐	☐	☐	☐	☐
	• I see the problems that I face in life and at work as challenges that I can solve.	☐	☐	☐	☐	☐	☐
6. Interpersonal Competence	• In social interactions at work and in my personal life, I am usually able to laugh at myself when appropriate.	☐	☐	☐	☐	☐	☐
	• I find it easy to empathize with others' frustrations, hurts, joys, misfortunes, and successes.	☐	☐	☐	☐	☐	☐

Resilience Facet	Sample Measurement Statements	Rating 1	2	3	4	5	6
7. Socially Connected	• I have a diverse group of people whom I consider good friends.	☐	☐	☐	☐	☐	☐
	• I find it easy to form lasting friendships.	☐	☐	☐	☐	☐	☐
8. Proactive	• I view change—even difficult and challenging change—as an opportunity for me to learn and grow.	☐	☐	☐	☐	☐	☐
	• When an unwelcome change is forced upon me, I can usually find a way to either influence the course of the change or find a way to make the change work for me on my terms.	☐	☐	☐	☐	☐	☐

Think About This

The noted American theologian Reinhold Niebuhr offered his famous "Serenity Prayer" in 1932 as a way to help people focus on their own actions to improve their situations or their outlook:

God give me the serenity to accept things which cannot be changed;
Give me courage to change things which must be changed;
And the wisdom to distinguish one from the other.

Although the primary responsibility for strengthening resilience lies with the individual, change leaders can help facilitate its development. Some suggested leader actions for helping others strengthen their resilience are listed in table 7-5.

Getting It Done

This chapter introduced the concept of resilience as a powerful ally in your effort to introduce and lead a change initiative in your organization. You also learned the various components that make up resilience and the importance of assessing resilience as a precursor for encouraging its development in others.

Table 7-4. Ten actions to develop your own resilience.

1. *Make connections.* Building strong relationships with others, seeking help from and providing help to others, and being active in community, social, and faith-based groups are all ways to strengthen your social connections.
2. *Avoid seeing crises as insurmountable problems.* You can't easily change the circumstances that you're in, but you can change how you *frame* these circumstances in your own mind. Try to look beyond the immediate crisis and toward a successful outcome. Look for positive signs and trends that demonstrate positive movement or results.
3. *Accept that change is part of living.* Accept that you may not be able to work the way that you would prefer to work or that achieving certain goals may no longer be possible.
4. *Move toward your goals.* Set realistic, attainable goals and then take small steps every day toward these goals. Instead of focusing on tasks that seem beyond reach, ask yourself, "What is one thing that I can accomplish today that moves me toward my goals?"
5. *Take decisive action.* Rather than hoping and wishing that the big problems will go away, do something direct and specific that engages you in these issues. Confront these issues head-on, and watch your sphere of influence and effectiveness grow.
6. *Look for opportunities for self-discovery.* Loss, injury, and pain, despite the hardship that they create for us, also contain kernels of insight, strength, and opportunity. Strive to find at least one positive result or outcome from the challenges you face now or soon will face. Can you find the silver lining in the dark cloud?
7. *Nurture a positive view of yourself.* Believe in your capacities to deal effectively with any issue that you face. Have confidence in your ability to overcome the odds and solve a difficult problem. Learn to trust your instincts.
8. *Keep things in perspective.* No matter how dark the present is and the future may appear, take a long view and see the current and future challenge within a larger context. Identify what *isn't* changing for you and remind yourself of the opportunities that may be opened up by the change. (See #6 above.)
9. *Maintain a hopeful outlook.* It's easy to focus on the negative and get depressed by an uncertain future and an overwhelming change. Avoid the temptation to wallow in being a victim of circumstances. Focus on what you want to achieve in this situation. Shift your orientation toward a positive and optimistic outcome and what you need to do to help achieve that outcome.
10. *Take care of yourself.* How are you feeling about the change? Are you anxious, afraid, uncertain, confused? Acknowledge your feelings and try to address them. Take time to do things that you find satisfying and relaxing. No matter how much work is on your plate, take a break, go for a walk, talk to a friend, or learn how to meditate or calm yourself. This will not only help you more effectively cope with the stressors and challenges, but also it will increase the quality of your thinking and your contributions.

Adapted from American Psychological Association. (2004). "The Road to Resilience." Washington, D.C.: American Psychological Association. http://helping.apa.org/featuredtopics/feature.php?id=6.

Table 7-5. Leader actions to help strengthen resilience in others.

- *Remind people what* isn't *changing.* There's a good chance that most of their work life won't change a bit. Help them keep the change in perspective.
- *Increase opportunities for social connections.* Host pizza parties, after work get-togethers, and celebration breaks to highlight key milestones being accomplished.
- *Increase communication about the coming changes and challenges.* Keep the information flowing, making sure that you use multiple modes: face-to-face, memos, emails, conference calls, meetings, and so forth to connect with people in a way that ensures that they understand where the organization is going and their role in this future.
- *Work hard to shift grousing and whining toward problem solving.* Allow 10 minutes of pure whining before shifting the focus by asking, "What can you do about this?" and related questions.
- *Listen to people's anxieties and fears.* When people express their fears about the change, say, "Tell me more." When they appear anxious, ask them to tell you what is concerning them. Then, pay attention when they start talking.
- *Acknowledge their losses.* Be upfront about the potential downsides of the change. Be honest about what will change, and then help people see the hidden opportunities that the change presents. Give people time to grieve what they may be giving up, and then help them see a better future.
- *Engage staff in developing a shared vision of a realistically optimistic future.* Don't just focus on *your* vision for the change, ask people about *their* ideas for solving the original problem and for meeting the challenges ahead. And make sure that you listen to and integrate, where possible, their ideas into the change design.
- *Encourage a healthy work-life balance.* During a change, stress levels climb along with workloads. Monitor the stress levels and make sure that people are taking time for themselves. Occasionally crunch time can require taking a shorter lunch break; as a rule, however, make sure that people are taking a physical break from the office for lunch whenever possible.
- *Hold brown-bag seminars.* Consider lunch-time seminars on health, wellness, stress management, taking care of yourself, and so on. Giving people information on self-management, stress relief, and being proactive puts them in charge of their own resilience.
- *Promote the employee assistance program.* Make sure people know about the services available to them. If your organization doesn't have an EAP, contact your human resources department to set one up.
- *Explain the "whys" of the change and associated challenges.* This isn't a new requirement for the change leader, but it's useful to know that understanding the "whys" can help people put the change in perspective and help them see a role for themselves in the change.
- *Celebrate the little victories along the way.* People need to know that their hard work is paying off and that the organization is moving forward. You can help strengthen resilience and build commitment to the change by pointing out to people that their actions are getting results.

(continued on page 118)

Table 7-5. Leader actions to help strengthen resilience in others (continued).

- *Keep the team together.* During a change, people can sometimes go off and focus on their narrow self-interest or dwell upon the insurmountable challenges before them. Work hard to keep people working in teams and work groups to tackle the challenges ahead *together.* Help people feel that they aren't in this alone and that by bringing people and ideas together they *will* find solutions that work.
- *Break problems or challenges into bite-sized pieces.* Big change projects can seem overwhelming and capable of eating people alive! Help people see that big, seemingly insurmountable tasks can be tackled by breaking them up into manageable pieces. People need to see and feel progress. Providing benchmarks that enable them to *feel* this progress will help keep their spirits high.
- *Model good practices and behaviors.* To lead change effectively, you need to at least be in the Inquiry, Experimentation, and Discovery phase of the emotional journey through change. (See chapter 5.) If you're in this phase, you have a forward-looking vision and want to see the change be successful. Use your positive mindset about the change to guide your daily practices and behaviors in support of the change. If, instead, you're in Fear, Anger, and Resistance, deal with your own issues first before attempting to help others with theirs.

Noted

Employee assistance programs (EAPs) provide confidential assistance to employees who are experiencing personal problems that may be interfering with their work performance. They function best when they help employees explore the personal options and strategies before them and assist them in making healthy choices from among these alternatives. Within the context of change, EAPs have proven to be especially effective at helping employees make choices that steer away from counterproductive behaviors, such as exhibiting passive-aggressive behaviors, getting even, undercutting the actions of others, abusing alcohol and other drugs, and even destroying property.

Change leaders should work closely with EAP professionals to support them in helping people find productive pathways for channeling their anxieties and fears. Because EAP professionals play an objective role in working to help both the employee and the organization, they can also help facilitate brown-bag sessions on dealing with stress from the change and could even be enlisted to facilitate proactive question-and-answer discussions about the coming change.

Now it's your turn to identify ways that you can assess, develop, and strengthen your own resilience and the resilience of others. Exercise 7-1 asks you to first assess your own resilience by reviewing each of the eight resilience dimensions and then identifying specific actions you will take to strengthen your resilience.

Exercise 7-1. Assessing and developing your resilience.

Assessing Your Resilience

Review the eight resilience dimensions. In the "strength" column, place a check mark for those dimensions that you believe to be your strongest and, in the "areas for improvement" column, place a check mark to indicate dimensions that might need strengthening.

Resilience Dimension	Strength (✓)	Area for Improvement (✓)
1. Self-Assurance	☐	☐
2. Personal Meaning and Vision	☐	☐
3. Flexible and Adaptable	☐	☐
4. Organized	☐	☐
5. Problem Solver	☐	☐
6. Interpersonal Competence	☐	☐
7. Socially Connected	☐	☐
8. Proactive	☐	☐

Developing Your Resilience

Based upon your self-assessment of the eight dimensions of your resilience, identify the steps and actions you will take to enhance, strengthen, and develop your resilience. Feel free to borrow from the ideas offered in table 7-4.

Exercise 7-2 turns your focus to the employees in your organization. Although only they can develop and strengthen their own resilience, there are actions you and other change leaders can take (a few of these are summarized in table 7-5) to encourage its development.

Exercise 7-2. Assessing and developing resilience in others.

Assessing Others' Resilience

Review the eight resilience dimensions. In the "strength" column, place a check mark for those dimensions that you believe to be the strongest for your team/work area. Then, in the "areas for improvement" column, place a check mark next to those dimensions that need strengthening for your team/work area.

Resilience Dimension	Strength (✓)	Area for Improvement (✓)
1. Self-Assurance	☐	☐
2. Personal Meaning and Vision	☐	☐
3. Flexible and Adaptable	☐	☐
4. Organized	☐	☐
5. Problem Solver	☐	☐
6. Interpersonal Competence	☐	☐
7. Socially Connected	☐	☐
8. Proactive	☐	☐

Developing Your Resilience

Based upon your assessment of your team or work area's strength in each of the eight resilience dimensions, identify the steps and actions you will take to help enhance, strengthen, and develop the resilience of your team/work area. Feel free to borrow from the ideas offered in table 7-5.

Becoming more resilient as a leader and working to strengthen resilience in others will help smooth the path of change. Without a thoughtful plan for leading the change, however, the road ahead will likely be a bumpy one. Chapter 8, the final chapter of this book, brings together the various elements explored throughout *Change Basics* into an integrative plan for leading (and managing) the change you are seeking to implement in your organization. Your change plan will provide you a roadmap to put you on the right road to a successful change outcome. So, let's start putting your plan together.

8

Developing Your Change Plan

What's Inside This Chapter

In this chapter you'll learn:

- The value of developing a formal plan for implementing your change initiative
- The steps for implementing a change
- How to use appreciative inquiry to identify organizational assets that your change initiative can draw upon as you move toward implementation
- Actions that change leaders should take to protect the change implementation plan.

The Value of Developing a Formal Change Implementation Plan

At this point in our exploration of the basic rules and approaches to managing and leading change, you should have a good sense of the nature and characteristic of change (chapter 1), the forces that are driving change in your organization today (chapter 2), your organization's relative readiness and receptivity for change (chapter 3), the four-phase model for introducing change (chapter 4), and the emotional journey that people follow when change is introduced (chapter 5). You should also have a good understanding of why people might resist change and how you can move them out of resistance (chapter 6) and, finally, you should have a better understanding of the role that resilience plays in how people respond to change and some ideas about how to build and strengthen resilience in yourself and others (chapter 7).

The previous chapters have given you a good map of the landscape of change and the change process. What you need now is a plan—a plan that ties together these interrelated elements into a thoughtful, comprehensive, and successful implementation strategy. The value of a step-by-step approach is that it helps ensure that you don't rush too quickly through the process or skip a critical step along the way.

Basic Rule 32

A thoughtful and planned approach for implementing change increases the probability of your success at leading change. It slows you down and challenges you to ask the right questions.

Developing a plan to implement change is important because it can

- slow your thinking down to ensure that you have thought through key steps of the leading change process
- clarify your thinking about what you want to accomplish through the change—your desired change outcomes, objectives, and measures
- require you to anticipate and prepare for the tough questions that you will inevitably have to address
- compel you to consider the effects and consequences of change
- help you develop a method for measuring the progress of your change initiative.

Nearly every successful change initiative begins with a plan. Yes, your change plan will itself undergo a change as you move it forward, but you need to begin with a framework that compels you to ask the right questions of the right people at the right time. Developing this plan is the focus of this chapter.

The Steps for Change Implementation

Leading change in your organization involves a deep understanding of the characteristics of change itself, your change vision and your change objectives, and the characteristics and potential reactions of those who are being asked to change. When the change is transformational in nature, meaning that it calls for a revolution in the way people think and act in the organization, the leaders of change must have an even deeper awareness of the complex issues involved in moving people from one state or condition to another.

Figure 8-1 highlights the range of issues that must be mastered to successfully implement change:

- understanding the nature of change as a disruptive yet positive force in people's lives and how it is integral to the learning, health, and longevity of an organization, and the consequences of not changing
- taking an inventory of the forces for change and identifying the potential impacts of these forces on various components within your organization
- clarifying your change vision—what you wanted the change to accomplish for customers, employees, and the organization as a whole
- learning how the change process works and what you must do to guide people through the process
- identifying the potential negative impacts of the change on stakeholders (employees, customers, suppliers, and so forth) and the reasons people might resist the new ideas and approaches brought about by the change
- understanding and managing the emotional transitions of change and identifying methods for developing commitment and resilience.

This chapter presents a framework to help you move from your own personal awareness of the need for change to creating conditions within your organization that enable the change to take hold. As you learned in chapter 3, the track record for change implementation in organizations is rather dismal, and you also learned some of the clear reasons behind these failures. Many of these causes stem from change leaders failing to anticipate and proactively engage the inevitable obstacles along the path toward change. The failures also stem from change leaders failing to think clearly and carefully about both what needs to happen in their organizations and how to develop stakeholder commitment to the new direction.

Figure 8-1. A framework for successfully introducing and leading change.

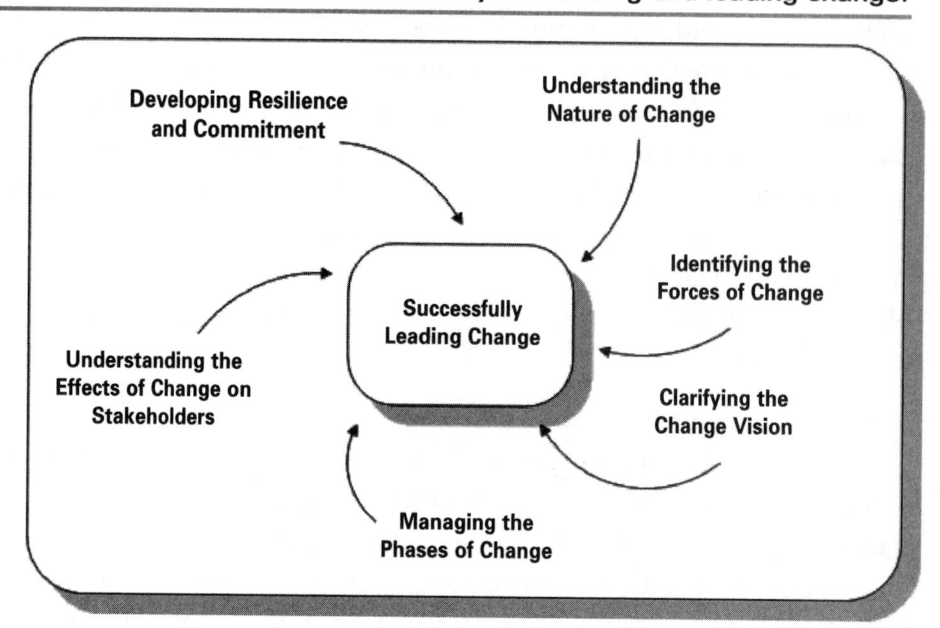

The framework for implementing change presented in this book involves one central tenet that is the basis for its proven success: Don't just do something, sit there! Slowing down the change process is a call for critical and thoughtful reflection before you begin pushing your organization in another direction. Before you rush to implement what you might view as a minor change, consider that for many in your organization that minor change may be more transformational than incremental. By following the framework offered in this chapter, you can avoid many of the mistakes made by others when introducing change, while improving your chance of success.

Basic Rule 33

Don't just do something, sit there! Stated otherwise, think before you act when leading change.

Developing Your Change Implementation Plan

Introducing change is not a linear process. It is a circular process in which you:

1. Put your plan together and roll out the plan.
2. Address the issues and questions that need to be addressed as the plan unfolds.
3. As your actions work or don't work, new issues arise, or you uncover new information, adjust and revise your plan accordingly.

Basic Rule 34

Planning change involves a circular process: develop and implement your plan, monitor progress and identify things that worked and those that didn't, and integrate changes into and revise your plan.

There are 10 key steps in the change implementation planning process. These steps, highlighted in table 8-1, capture the most important factors you need to consider as you move to protect your organization's future. The rest of this chapter identifies the issues that should be integrated into each of these 10 steps.

Step 1: Identify the Need for Change

As you learned in chapter 4, the first component of a successful change implementation plan is identifying the need for change. A multitude of forces within and outside of your organization have, to varying extents, a present or future influence over your organization's future. Many of these internal or external forces have little effect on what your organization does today or tomorrow. A few, however, are destined to have a dramatic and transformational effect on your organization. For some reason, you have sensed a need for your organization to change. Some of these driving forces have captured your attention and created a felt need for change. What was it that got your attention? What information caught your eye and caused you to begin thinking of the need for an alternative future for your team or organization?

This first step in the planning process is simply identifying and documenting the forces for change as you understand them and—most important—the business case driving the change initiative. This also involves identifying the various aspects of your organization that are affected and the degree of change that may be required. Is the change incremental (affecting only a few people in small ways), or is it transformational (affecting many people in profound ways)? Every change begins

Table 8-1. Components of a change implementation plan.

Steps of the Change Implementation Plan	Questions to Consider
1. Identify the Need for Change	Why is there a need for change? Do people feel *urgency* about the change? What are the forces driving the change? What is the business case for the change?
2. Create a Leading Change Design Team	Who must be involved in helping you move your organization in a new direction? What internal work areas or departments should be involved in designing the change?
3. Inventory the Effects of the Forces for Change	What are the potential effects of the forces on the organization? What organizational components, departments, or work units in your organization are affected and to what degree? Do these forces suggest incremental or transformational change in the organization?
4. Define the Ideal State and Develop a Preliminary Vision for Change	What is the change that needs to occur? What will the outcomes of the change look like? What is really changing? How will you and others know if the change has been successful?
5. Identify the Effects of the Proposed Change	What are the pros and cons of the change? Who benefits and who loses? Are customers hurt as well as helped?
6. Assess Organizational Readiness for Change and Identify Organizational Assets to Support the Change	To what extent do people at all levels of the organization see the need for change? Will the organization's culture support or undercut the change? What existing organizational assets can be used to support the change and serve as building blocks for success?
7. Create Your Preliminary Strategy and Action Plan	How will you raise stakeholder awareness of the need for change? How will the losses be reduced, eliminated, or managed? How will stakeholders be involved in developing the change vision and strategy? What actions will build stakeholder commitment? How will you manage the transitions? What are the stakeholder benefits from the change? What is the implementation timeline? What benchmarks will help track progress?
8. Develop Your Communication Strategy	With your change plan in hand, before you implement you need to invest time upfront in developing a plan for strengthening communication throughout the change implementation process. Without a focused communication strategy, your change effort is likely to fail.
9. Implement the Change Plan	Commit resources, take actions, provide training, and purchase equipment to support the changes.
10. Monitor and Evaluate the Implementation Plan and Revise as Needed	Who will track progress? How will revisions be identified and integrated into the plan? When will measurement of results begin?

with a clear definition of why change is needed from a business perspective. Without a compelling business case, you may not be able to get the critical support for change from key stakeholders concerned about the organization's bottom line.

Noted

Every change is one of two types of change: incremental or transformational. Incremental change is everyday change that gradually nudges attitudes and behaviors in a new direction. Transformational change is change that radically redirects attitudes and behaviors in a direction that significantly veers from their present path.

An example of an incremental change might be adding an additional responsibility to someone's job description that slightly expands his or her job in a direction that is consistent with his or her existing duties and responsibilities. A transformational change might involve getting rid of job descriptions entirely and asking people to redefine their daily work around the strategic challenges facing the organization, the vision for the organization and their team/department, and the value-added competencies that they bring to their work.

It should be noted that there isn't usually a shared definition on a given change as to whether it is incremental or transformational. A change such as the redesign of the workflow on an existing production line might be viewed by one person on the line as incremental and logical and by the very next person in the line as a radical or transformational change. Change leaders never make assumptions about whether a change is incremental or transformational. They recognize that it's not how they themselves view the change, it's how those who are directly affected by the change define it.

Some important questions you need to answer in this initial phase of pulling your plan together include:

- What are the external forces that are driving the need for change?
- What are the internal forces that are driving the need for change?
- What are the business implications of these driving forces?
- What data on the organization's quality, cost, profitability, past success or failure, performance in relation to industry standards, and so forth suggest the need for change?

Step 2: Create a Leading Change Team

Step 2 of the process involves creating a leading change design team. You can't move your organization by yourself. Even if you happen to be on your organization's board of directors or the head of your department, you won't get far along the path of change without the ideas, energy, and behavior of others. Throughout *Change Basics,* you've read about how involving people at all phases of the change process is fundamental to the successful introduction of a change.

The leading change design team should comprise about eight to 10 others who, like yourself, have a keen awareness of the forces working within and outside of your organization. They should be people who care about the future of the organization, people who believe that its success can only be preserved if it anticipates and responds to the forces within and surrounding it. You might eventually invite those who will be the biggest resisters to help you design the change, but initially you want willing leaders.

You should create a diverse team of people who are dedicated to your organization and willing to confront the tough issues it faces. A diverse team means that it includes people who have widely divergent viewpoints, perspectives, and experiences, but who have a common commitment to the organization's future. You'll also want people representing different organizational departments, especially areas feeling the most pressure from the forces for change.

Your leading change design team should also include someone from your organization's executive leadership team. This executive sponsor of the change will play a key role on the team and in the organization. This individual provides organizational support for the change and, by helping to guide the change, demonstrates the executive leadership's commitment to moving ahead in this important area. And, especially when it comes to allocating and shifting resources around to support the change initiatives, this executive sponsor will play an essential role at sustaining the change.

With your leading change design team together and committed to moving your organization ahead, your next step is to revisit the forces for change in step one. You had to do some initial thinking on your own in step 1 to help you focus your mind on the issues facing your organization and to know who to initially invite into the design of the change. Now guide the leading change design team in developing and expanding upon these initial ideas. The information that the team gathers as it revisits step 1 will be used to help create a felt need or urgency in the organization (the first phase of the leading change model from chapter 4) and throughout the change process.

Step 3: Identify the Effects of the Change Forces

Step 3 builds on the inventory of the forces driving change by identifying the effects of these forces on the organization's departments, employees, customers, and the organization's future. In step 3, you and your design team assess who is affected by the forces driving change and the potential effects and consequences of these forces. The team will also identify the scale of the change that may be required to respond effectively to these forces. The team should find answers to such questions as:

- How do the forces that are driving this change affect the various departments, units, and components of the organization (such as purpose, leadership, structure, technology, behavior, systems, and culture)? *Note:* These organizational components were discussed in detail in chapter 2.
- How deeply do these forces cut into the heart of what the organization is and does?
- What specifically are the potential incremental or transformational effects of these forces for change on people?

Answers to these questions define what the team does next and what the change will look like as it moves into the organization.

At this point, the leading change designers haven't yet defined what the change will look like. All they've done is define the forces for change and their likely impact on the organization. They've also identified the type or degree of change warranted by the forces for change. Defining the actual change, including how it looks and feels, is the next step.

Step 4: Define the Ideal State and Develop a Preliminary Change Vision

Step 4 involves developing a preliminary change vision that is needed in response to the driving forces. In creating this preliminary vision, the design team begins with the organization's broader vision or purpose and then moves to describing the desired result or ideal state for the change. This ideal state or vision for the change should link to the organization's broader vision and should lead to something profoundly positive for the organization, its customers, and employees, while successfully confronting the threats from the forces of change. Because change for change's sake wastes the organization's resources and exhausts employees, the change should offer a clear and compelling solution to the pressing problems and challenges facing the organization.

Think About This

Making a business case for change is fundamental to a successful change effort. A change that isn't anchored to the fundamentals of the organization's business—profits, customer satisfaction, quality, efficiency, competitive pressure, the founder's vision, and so forth—won't survive the legitimate challenges that stakeholders of all types are likely to surface at the first word of change. Drawing a clear line and connection between the change vision and the fundamentals of the business gets people's attention, commands organizational resources, and relates to meaningful and measurable results.

The design team members first describe the desired ideal state for the organization and then plot out what, from their perspective, must happen within the organization to achieve that outcome. This step defines the "what" of the change. Some of the questions considered during this stage of the plan's development include:

- What aspect of the work done by employees or the outcomes experienced by customers is actually changing?
- In what way are these things changing?
- How is the current state different from the ideal state? What components of this current state will need to change? What is not in alignment with the ideal state?
- Is the change incremental or transformational?
- Are the jobs of employees transformed into something completely different or is the change simply a minor adjustment to what already exists?
- Will customers' relationship with the organization or employees be affected in any way?
- What is the business case for the change vision? How does this change vision address fundamental business issues (such as growth, profitability, cost reduction, product/service mix, competitive pressure, quality and productivity improvement, shareholder value)?
- What are the potential benefits of this change? How will employees and other stakeholders realize these benefits?
- What is the profoundly positive outcome that the change will help the organization realize?

- How does this change vision offer a better alternative future for the organization and its stakeholders than its present course of action?
- Will key stakeholders find this change vision compelling in articulating both the reasons for the change and the alternative future?

After the design team has answered these and related questions, the ideal and current states have been defined and the depth and degree of the change and the business case for the change are better understood. Perhaps for the first time the design team has a sense of the degree of the long-range implications of the change.

The last component of step four involves developing outcome measures that the design team, and eventually the entire organization, can use to assess whether the change was successful in achieving its objectives. Good performance measures can gauge the effectiveness of the change. They help keep the goals of the change in focus and are a powerful way to communicate expectations to employees.

Table 8-2 offers a few characteristics of effective outcome measures. When your team develops its plan for implementing the change, make sure that you make outcome measures an integral part of your design.

Table 8-2. Characteristics of effective measures.

Effective measures or metrics for a change initiative should:

- Measure progress on what matters most, particularly matters relating to the organization's vision, mission, core values, and strategic objectives
- Demonstrate improvement in a core business deliverable, such as profitability, waste reduction, cost reduction, quality improvement, and so forth
- Reflect the *results* from the change vs. the *activities* involved with implementation
- Be simple, understandable, and clear to people on the front line—the measure must have meaning to those who are doing the work
- Be linked to daily behaviors so people can see the relationship between what they do every day and the desired results
- Measure both *process* (the success of the *doing* and implementation of the change) and the *outcomes* or results from the change
- Reveal a cause → effect relationship between the *behaviors* of individuals/teams and the *outcomes* resulting from these behaviors
- Be few in number (no more than five to eight) to help people focus on the most critical issues
- Be the result of SMART goals (Specific, Measurable, Accepted by those who are expected to implement, Realistic, and Time-bound).

Step 5: Identify the Effects on Stakeholders

With the ideal state now more clearly defined, the design team moves to step 5: defining the effects of the change on employees, customers, shareholders, suppliers, and others. In this step, you assess the potential losses and negative impact that the change will have on employees and others. You also need to identify potential benefits and gains from the change and if these gains can be used as offsets to the potential losses. When considering the potential losses and gains from the change, you should consider such questions as:

- What is actually changing for people? What will they be asked to do differently? What isn't changing for them?
- Why should people embrace this change? What's in it for them?
- What can be done to increase the chances that the benefits of the change will be realized by those who are being asked to implement the change?
- Can the perceived losses be reduced or eliminated? For the losses that remain, can offsetting benefits be used to help sell this change?
- Who are the big losers with this change? What actions can you take to help this group embrace the change?
- What interim benefits might be available to provide positive incentives for people to work with you to move the change forward?

An important principle to consider during this stage of the planning process is the rule of unintended consequences. As discussed in chapter 1, the rule of unintended consequences suggests that what you hope will occur as a result of the proposed change *may* happen, but what you don't think or anticipate *will* happen. Keep this rule in mind as you think through the implications of each change you are proposing. For each aspect of your change design, consider such questions as:

- What is the intended purpose of this specific change? Do you have a clear understanding of the desired result?
- What could go wrong with implementing this aspect of the change if it is not done right?
- What potential unintended consequences might surface as you implement the change?

Step 6: Assess Organizational Readiness for Change and Identify Organizational Assets to Support the Change

At this point in the development of your change plan, you have some data on the need for change, some possible effects and consequences from the forces driving change, and you have sketched out a preliminary vision or ideal state for the change. Before you go any further toward implementation, this is a good time to slow down and gather data that are more complete from the organization beyond your design team.

One source of data that will help shape everything you do from here on out is the organizational change readiness assessment (exercise 3-3). This tool is a means for gathering information on the organization's relative change readiness. Now is the time to use this tool to gain some initial insights into how receptive the organization will be to yet another change. Distribute the tools to your design team members and a healthy sampling of others at all levels of the organization to give you a 360-degree perspective on change readiness.

So, you have some change readiness data in hand. Even with this data, however, you're not done with data collection. Before pulling your plan together, you and the other change leaders in your organization would benefit from a fresh approach and an even deeper perspective on your organization, the challenges it faces, and the assets that the organization brings to these challenges. At this point in the plan development process, you should use a specific approach for gathering critical data from all levels of the organization. This additional data will help build consensus around the need for change and help you identify organizational assets that may be essential to the organization's achieving its goals. The data gathered should also explore the deeper cultural assumptions that people hold about the organization and its future and their perceptions of the organization's strengths as it moves to adopt a significant change.

As you begin formulating the questions you will ask in your interviews, you can use a process that borrows heavily from a process called appreciative inquiry, a powerful technique developed by David Cooperrider in the 1980s that seeks to identify and leverage the organization's strengths and capabilities. Cooperrider asserts that it is these assets that will enable an organization to prepare for and respond to its current and future challenges. If you use a method to understand these organizational strengths, your change implementation design and strategy is likely to be more successful because it is anchored to the organization's assets and capabilities. When you focus on strengths, assets, and opportunities—not just upon creating a felt need for change—you strengthen your change implementation plan.

Noted

Appreciative inquiry, as defined by Cooperrider, is grounded upon two key assumptions. The first, and most important, is that organizations are sustained by what they do well, their strengths, their successes, and by the affirmative contributions that employees at all levels of the organization make toward the organization's success. The second assumption is that the nature of an inquiry itself—the kinds of questions that you ask and how you ask them—influences how the individuals in the organization respond. Hence, by exploring the organization's strengths in your inquiry, you will not only identify that which gives it life, but also begin the subtle and positive shift of perspective toward an affirmative change process.

According to Cooperrider, Whitney, and Stavros (2003, p. 3), appreciative inquiry is the "cooperative and co-evolutionary search for the best in people, their organizations, and the world around them. It involves the discovery of what gives 'life' to a living system when it is most effective, alive, and constructively capable in economic, ecological, and human terms."

A comprehensive appreciative inquiry process, which can involve dozens if not hundreds of interviews and includes both small and large group processes, can be a powerful foundation for the organization's change initiatives. The results from appreciative inquiry can, and in fact should, end up driving key change strategies largely because of the participatory discovery process used and the rich reservoir of knowledge that often lies buried in the organization. Although time constraints and resource limitations may limit the scope of your appreciative inquiry method and process, using a modified process that is modeled on the appreciative inquiry method can still be a powerful tool to help facilitate the change. Although you won't glean all the benefits available through the more expansive process, what you learn from a more focused effort can and should play an important role in the development of the overall change implementation plan.

In-depth interviews with key stakeholders involved in or affected by the change process can help you explore the diversity of issues that make up organizational readiness for change and identify important organizational assets that the change can leverage and build upon as the change is implemented. During these structured one-on-one interviews, you will have the opportunity to explore the mindsets of the respondents as well as the organizational context issues of culture and the respondents' perceptions of the organization's history with change.

At a minimum, you should plan on interviewing a significant sample of those stakeholders who are leading the change process and those who are likely to be affected by the upcoming change. You also, however, should dig deeper into the organization by talking with a diverse sample of managers, supervisors, team leaders, and staff at every level of the organization. The point of your interviews is to discover how these diverse players view the organization and its capacities for dealing with organizational change. You will also have the opportunity to assess the mindset of these key players in the process and their perceptions of the organization's culture and practices as they relate to change and its implementation.

Each of your interviews should be structured such that the same questions are asked of all participants. See table 8-3 for some possible questions to explore in each appreciative inquiry interview. Each interview should last no more than an hour and should provide an opportunity for participants to offer their thoughts both in response to your questions and to offer additional thoughts in the context of the interview's focus. Following the interviews, you should summarize the results by noting the main themes and trends that surface from your discussions.

The results from the organizational readiness assessment and the appreciative inquiry questions will help you identify the challenges you face and the organizational assets to build upon when initiating and designing your change implementation plan and strategy. These appreciative inquiry questions can lead you to some powerful insights into the organization's culture, practices, and behaviors in relation to organizational change generally and to the stated change objective specifically. These insights, in turn, can be used by you and others as building blocks for creating a successful change implementation plan.

Step 7: Create Your Preliminary Strategy and Action Plan

Step 7, developing your preliminary change strategy and action plan, is the stage in which the design team

- develops its initial ideas for the specific changes that need to take place
- identifies who is responsible for making these changes

Table 8-3. Sample questions for an appreciative inquiry interview about change.

1. Reflect back upon this organization's history of dealing with externally or internally driven change. Tell me a story or cite an incident where, from your perspective, this organization effectively and powerfully engaged in and effectively implemented a major change.
   a. What enabled the change implementation plan to go so well?
   b. What did the key players (stakeholders) do that enabled this successful outcome?
   c. What was it about the climate in the organization (or its subunit) that supported, reinforced, and sustained these change implementation efforts?
2. From your perspective, what do you see as the overarching vision for this organization? What is the profoundly positive difference we should strive to make in the world? How far are we from achieving this vision today?
3. What do you see as the most important strategic and operational challenges facing the organization and which, if they are not addressed, might prevent us from achieving our vision?
4. What strengths does this organization have in its strategic thinking, planning, decision making, problem solving, and change implementation capabilities that will enable it to meet these challenges? How have these strengths been expressed or how are they evident/visible in the organization?
5. What core values should govern the way that this organization engages in strategic thinking, planning, decision making, and implementing change?
6. What do you think is the "life-giving" factor, value, or characteristic that enables this organization to pull through during difficult times and changes?
7. How could this organization build upon its strengths, core values, and life-giving factors to enable it to meet successfully the future challenges you identified and help it to achieve its vision for the future?
   a. What current practices might this organization strengthen or develop to enable it to understand and effectively respond to the challenges ahead and achieve its change vision?
8. Imagine that it is one year from now and this organization has successfully implemented the changes that it has needed to make.
   a. How did the organization achieve this goal?
   b. How did the change process engage key stakeholders (leaders, staff, customers, suppliers, and others)?
   c. How were fears, objections, anxieties, concerns, and questions dealt with along the way?
   d. How did people work together at all levels of this organization to make the change relevant and engaging?
   e. As a result of this positive change to the organization, how are people working, communicating, interacting, deciding, planning, and collaborating differently from the way they used to?
9. If I were to grant you three wishes that, if fulfilled, would help the organization achieve its successful and transformative change objectives, what would those three wishes be?
10. Is there anything else that you'd like to share with me that you think might benefit our efforts to help build a great organization by moving toward our future vision?

- documents the impacts of the changes on the organizational subsystems
- defines the methods for involving stakeholders in designing the change
- develops strategies for increasing commitment to the change, and reducing the perceived losses and other negative effects.

As part of this step, you and the design team should anticipate who is most likely to resist the change, identify the origins of their resistance, and develop strategies to reduce or eliminate the causes of resistance. Your change strategy and action should address the list of issues identified in table 8-4.

Table 8-4. Issues to address in creating your change strategy.

Make sure you include the following when developing your strategy and actions for implementing your change:

- *Awareness and change readiness:* Your ideas for raising stakeholder awareness of the need for change and actions you will take to develop and enhance change readiness. This might involve working to shape your organizational culture to support the proposed changes—a process that itself requires a *cultural* change plan.
- *Involvement:* The actions you will take to involve stakeholders in developing a *shared vision,* establishing goals for the change, refining the change strategy and actions, and defining performance measures. Include ideas for involving the stakeholders who are most affected by the change in designing how their jobs or roles will change and in creating their own futures.
- *Support for the change from managers and supervisors:* Your frontline supervisors and managers know your organization best. They have a good sense of what will fly with the frontline staff and what won't. Listen to them, build into your plan ample opportunities for these key stakeholders to voice their issues, concerns, questions, anxieties, and fears, and then do your best to respond to them. If members of this group aren't at least in the Inquiry, Experimentation, and Discovery phase of the journey through change, they won't be willing or able to sell the change to the people on the front line.
- *Political support for change:* How will you get the attention of the leadership? What is the depth and extent of top leadership support for this change? Identify the steps you'll take to get full leadership support of the initiative. Who on the leadership team might sponsor this change initiative?
- *Linkage with the organization's vision and strategy:* Address how the change advances the organization's vision, links with its existing strategy, and meets core business requirements. Alternatively, identify how the existing vision, strategy, or business requirements will need to be modified or adjusted.
- *Resistance:* Identify the stakeholders who will very likely resist the change, why they may resist, and how you will address these causes of their resistance.
- *Commitment:* What are your methods for developing stakeholder commitment to the change? What investments in training, equipment, reward system changes, or other structural changes in the organization will you make to reinforce stakeholder commitment to the change?

(continued on page 140)

Table 8-4. Issues to address in creating your change strategy (continued).

- *Transitions:* Define the actions you will take to manage the emotional *transitions* of both the endings (what people are leaving behind and giving up) and the new beginnings (what people will be starting or learning). What ceremonies, rituals, and celebrations will you initiate to help recognize and respond to people's emotional needs during change?
- *Communication:* What are your approaches for communicating with all stakeholders regarding the change vision, goals, and strategy? *Note:* This issue will be more fully developed in the next step in developing your change implementation plan.
- *Implications:* Identify the short- and long-term implications of the change on the organization's departments, structure, customer relationships, and other organizational aspects and how each will be addressed.
- *Resources:* Identify the resource commitments the organization will need to make to implement the change successfully. Resources might include training, tools, equipment, purchasing authority, access to information, and so forth that will be required to support and sustain the new behaviors.
- *Monitoring and evaluating:* Develop ideas for monitoring, measurement, evaluation, and revision of the plan.
- *Benchmarks:* Along with methods for monitoring and evaluating the progress of your change initiative, establish clear benchmarks and a timeline for implementation that enables you and others to gauge the success of the change.

Build your plan carefully. Involve your frontline managers and supervisors in every aspect of the design process. Know what success looks like and make sure that your plan identifies the way that you'll track success. This step of the process should reflect the best thinking in your organization and a thoughtful awareness of how to introduce change in an organization.

Before you move to implement, however, you'll need to invest considerable time and effort in the next step—building a communication strategy that helps keep the change moving forward.

Step 8: Develop a Communication Strategy to Support the Change Plan

As noted throughout this book, the quality of your communications during the change can make or break your initiative. Step 8 of your change implementation plan involves developing a more detailed strategy for communicating with key stakeholders throughout all phases of the leading change process.

What are the consequences if you don't have a communication strategy? Table 8-5 lists only a few of the negative consequences and implications when you seek to implement a change without a supporting communication strategy.

Basic Rule 35

The quality and frequency of your communication during change is a defining factor in the success or failure of your change initiative.

Table 8-5. The consequences of not having a communication strategy.

Communication is vital to the success of every organizational change. Poorly managed communications during a change process can lead to such organizational outcomes as: • Confusion as to the reasons for the change • Higher levels of resistance • Increased levels of uncertainty and fear • Higher levels of employee anxiety about the future • Greater levels of mistrust of management and change leaders • Confusion about the new expectations • An erosion in a sense of community • Reduction in employee readiness to accept change • An organizational incapacity to adjust or modify the change based upon the wisdom of the organization • Missed opportunities • Lack of understanding of the change's progress • Doubt about whether the change has led to the desired effects or results.

Your communication strategy to support the change initiative plays a central role in reinforcing the key actions of leaders throughout the four-phase leading change model. The strategy also helps those who are being asked to change to understand the whys of change, the change vision, where they fit into the future of the organization, what they need to do to make the change happen, and how they will know that the organization is making progress with the change.

If you design your communication strategy right, it will also provide you and other change leaders with important insights into employee concerns, reservations, issues, questions, and challenges. It will provide a vehicle for gathering employee ideas and perspectives that, once integrated into the change, will strengthen the change initiative.

Table 8-6 identifies an array of communication requirements that your communication strategy will need to address for each of the four phases of the leading change model (from chapter 4).

Step 9: Implement the Plan

Step 9 of your change implementation plan involves moving ahead with your comprehensive plan. This, of course, is far from simple. Moving ahead means having conviction and courage in the face of the resistance you expect and the resistance you didn't expect. Moving ahead means enduring—and surviving—criticism of your challenge to the status quo, the nature and quality of your solutions, the implementation timeline, the incentives to help build support for the change, and just about every other aspect of your change plan that you have painstakingly pulled together.

Leading a major change initiative is not for the faint of heart. At least initially, until you can guide people into the Inquiry, Experimentation, and Discovery phase (covered in chapter 5), you will likely have more people working against the change to keep it from happening than you will have working with you to make it happen. At first, the feedback you will likely get from the organization is that everything about the change initiative is wrong and won't work. Have patience. Focus on your plan and persevere.

If you have designed your change initiative well, you and the others involved in helping frame and give birth to this change will have anticipated many of these objections and concerns. Expect resistance and expect to still be surprised at the strength of the pushback and where the pushback may be coming from. The rule of unintended consequences practically guarantees that things won't go as planned and that you may end up with more or perhaps less than what you expected.

Conviction and courage during the implementation stage are especially needed from your organization's top leaders. They must be prepared to commit the time and resources to the effort to see the change through. They should be prepared to defend the change with stakeholders—employees, customers, suppliers, and others—who may believe that the change is unnecessary and even harmful to the organization. In the early days of any change, even a change that is thoughtfully planned, you are likely to encounter stiff resistance, some of it expected and much of it unexpected. Prepare the top leadership for this painful beginning. Tell them to expect to feel the heat, the resistance, and the negative reactions. Lead them through a discussion of the painful consequences of not changing. (See chapter 2.)

Table 8-6. Communication requirements throughout the change process.

Phase of Change	Communication Requirements
Create a Felt Need	• Explain the reasons for the change. • Communicate key performance indicators suggesting a need for change. • Highlight the forces in the external environment putting pressure on the organization. • Identify what needs to change. • Define the organizational and personal consequences of not changing.
Introduce the Change	• Describe the change vision. • Describe what the effects of the proposed change will be. • Communicate the inevitability of the change. • Hear employee issues, questions, concerns, fears, and so forth. • Communicate empathy and understanding for anxieties, losses, fear, and other concerns. • Hear employee ideas, solutions, and strategies for strengthening the change.
Revise and Finalize the Change Vision	• Continue sharing the change vision as it changes and evolves. • Define boundaries within which people can explore solutions and be creative. • Listen for emerging obstacles and objections. • Communicate specific changes made to the change based upon employee input. • Tell and show employees how the change has evolved. • Communicate the progress of the change. • Celebrate interim accomplishments. • Express confidence in employees' abilities. • Communicate roles and expectations during the transition. • Celebrate/communicate key milestones and interim deliverables.
Stabilize and Sustain the Change	• Acknowledge the hard work done by those who made the change happen. • Publicize and celebrate the success of the change. • Publish new organizational charts, job descriptions, performance goals, and so forth. • Educate or train employees and others on the new procedures or processes. • Publish/communicate methods the organization will be using to reinforce new procedures and behaviors. • Communicate the need for ongoing changes. • Continue sharing organizational performance data (for example, customer satisfaction, costs, profitability, quality).

Basic Rule 36

A change initiative rises or falls based upon the depth of commitment to the change by the executive leadership and the degree of sustained support they demonstrate by providing sufficient time, money, material, human, and other resources required to see the change through.

The good news is that you won't experience only pushback and resistance. You may find that many people at all levels of the organization are ready for the change and willing to do whatever it takes to make the change work. Take advantage of these early adopters and work with them on their teams to help move the change forward. Provide ample opportunity for them to share their ideas, issues, questions, and concerns about the change and then, as with those who are resisting the change, integrate what you learn from these ground-level change champions into the change.

Think About This

The early adopters and those who demonstrate early leadership of the change, regardless of their official role in the organization, are the change leader's greatest assets and allies. When others—perhaps even you—are harboring deep reservations and concerns about the change, these forward-looking agents can help you find and sustain the much needed energy to keep the change idea alive.

They may be few in number, but they are an important backstop to help prevent the organization from slipping backward into yesterday's comfort and control. Early on in your change initiative, identify these early adopters and budding change champions. Encourage them. Develop them. Reward and reinforce them. Use them as advocates for the change among those on the front line. They may carry more street credibility than you do and can also help gather data about needed improvements to the change vision and strategy.

Some important questions to consider in this step in your plan development include these:

- Where are you encountering the most resistance? What might be behind this pushback?
- What adjustments might you make to the plan to accommodate surprising sources of resistance or support?

- How are your managers and other leaders dealing with the change? What provisions have you made to enlist their support and commitment to the new direction?
- How are you measuring progress? By the clock? By the level of resistance? By hitting key milestones and deliverables?
- How well is your communication strategy working at engaging people at all levels of the organization in understanding and supporting the change?

Whatever the response from the organization, keep the change moving forward. Based on the pushback and on the ideas and suggestions you get from both the resisters and the change champions along the way, you will be making numerous adjustments to your change vision and strategy. As demonstrated with the leading change model, your change will strengthen to the extent that you listen to and integrate into the change plan the ideas of others and what you are learning as the change unfolds, which brings us to the final step of your change implementation plan: step 10.

Step 10: Monitor, Evaluate, and Adjust the Change Plan

This, the final step of your change implementation plan, kicks into gear at the same time as step 9. At the point when you begin implementation you should also have the systems and infrastructures in place to measure and track progress, identify what's working and not working about the plan, and mechanisms to make adjustments and revisions to the plan. A plan that fails to design in mechanisms for monitoring, evaluation, and adjustment quickly becomes static and irrelevant.

A good plan will change as you, the design team, and other stakeholders collect information, make decisions, try out and abandon or integrate new ideas, and discover new insights into causes or potential solutions. The questions that concern you in this stage include:

- How is the change being received?
- Are we hitting key milestones, benchmarks, and deliverable dates?

Basic Rule 37

Before you implement your change, ensure that you have reinforcing systems and infrastructure to help you measure and track progress and, most important, to reward people for doing things the new way.

- Are we seeing positive results?
- Is the design team meeting regularly to review progress and make adjustments to the change vision, strategy, and plan?
- Have you communicated changes made to the change plan to all stakeholder groups?
- Have you communicated small successes and little victories along the way?
- Do people feel that progress is being made and that the organization is recognizing their hard work?

The most useful change plan is one that helps people make decisions and take actions in the present, keeping in mind the change vision and its promises. To provide this direction and support to decision making and action, your plan must include within itself routine checks to ensure that it is still relevant. Revising the plan based upon these periodic checks is essential to its success.

Now It's Up to You!

This chapter has outlined a detailed framework for creating a thoughtful plan to guide your change vision into and throughout your organization. Just the act of creating a plan has forced you to look deep into the heart of the change you believe needs to happen. It has compelled you to think in a formal way about the outcomes you want to see from the change, how people are likely to be affected by the change, and the actions you and others in your organization should take to make the change a reality.

Having a good plan, of course, doesn't guarantee that the change will happen. There will be many bumps along the path toward success. By developing a thoughtful plan, however, you and the leading change design team will have anticipated likely obstacles. You will have done your best to prevent or effectively deal with them before they derail your efforts.

Leading change in your organization is not a destination, it's a journey. Arriving at the destination may never happen simply because, just as you are settling into the

Basic Rule 38

Leading change is a journey, not a destination.

groove of a completed change project, a new need for change is surfacing in somebody else's mind somewhere in your organization. Regardless of its origins, however, change and the need for change are two of the few constants in your organization and in your own career as an HRD and OD professional.

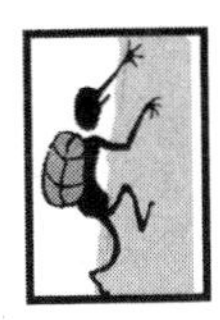

Getting It Done

The final chapter of *Change Basics* has been an integrative one that pulled together the various strands of thought and exploration about change into a 10-step process for developing your change plan. It's now your turn to identify your next steps in pulling together your plan.

Exercise 8-1 asks you to define your role in planning and facilitating your organization's change process.

Exercise 8-1. Defining your role in the leading change plan.

Your Role in the Change Plan and Facilitating Acceptance of the Change

Identify the role that you will play in developing and facilitating the change plan and in helping to facilitate acceptance of the change. If you are an HRD professional, how will your training and development role aid the development of the change plan and assist with implementation? If you work in an OD capacity, how can you best support the change initiative?

Exercise 8-2 is an opportunity to reflect upon the 10-step process introduced in this chapter and to plan your next steps in developing your strategy for introducing change in your organization.

Exercise 8-2. Prework involved in identifying next steps for developing your leading change plan.

For each of the 10 steps involved in developing your organization's change implementation plan, identify specific prework that will need to be accomplished to successfully complete that particular step. For example, in step 2, identify prospective members of the design team, and for step 6, identify individuals to complete the change readiness assessment and those who will be interviewed as part of the appreciative inquiry interviews.

Steps in Developing the Change Plan	Prework to Help Accomplish this Step
1. Identify the Need for Change	
2. Create a Leading Change Design Team	
3. Inventory the Effects of the Forces for Change	
4. Define the Ideal State and Develop a Preliminary Vision for Change	
5. Identify the Effects of the Proposed Change	
6. Assess Organizational Readiness for Change and Identify Organizational Assets to Support the Change	
7. Create Your Preliminary Strategy and Action Plan	
8. Develop Your Communication Strategy	
9. Implement the Change Plan	
10. Monitor and Evaluate the Implementation Plan and Revise as Needed	

This book has guided you through the process required to successfully introduce a change in your organization. Whether the change facing your organization is incremental or transformational, the approaches and tools that you have learned in this book will increase your chances of achieving your "ideal state" change vision.

The next steps of moving forward with your change plan are up to you. Good luck on your journey!

References

American Psychological Association. (2004). "The Road to Resilience." Washington, D.C.: American Psychological Association. http://helping.apa.org/featuredtopics/feature.php?id=6.

Armenakis, A.A., S.G. Harris, and K.W. Mossholder. (1993). "Creating Readiness for Organizational Change." *Human Relations, 46*(6): 681–703.

Bernard, B. (1991). *Fostering Resiliency in Kids: Protective Factors in the Family, School, and Community.* Portland, OR: Northwest Regional Education Laboratory.

Bridges, W. (1991). *Managing Transitions.* Reading, MA: Addison-Wesley Publishing Company.

Brooks, R., and S. Goldstein. (2003). *The Power of Resilience: Achieving Balance, Confidence, and Personal Strength in Your Life.* New York: McGraw-Hill.

Cairns, R.B., and B.D. Cairns. (1995). *Lifelines and Risks: Pathways of Youth in Our Time.* Cambridge, England: Cambridge University Press.

Compact Oxford English Dictionary (1991). New York: Oxford University Press USA.

Conner, D.R. (1992). *Managing at the Speed of Change.* New York: Random House.

Cooperrider, D., D. Whitney, and J.M. Stavros. (2003). *Appreciative Inquiry Handbook.* Bedford Heights, OH, and San Francisco, CA: Lakeshore Communications and Berrett-Koehler.

Dalai Lama XIV. (1998). *The Four Noble Truths.* London, England: Thorsons.

Dunham, R. (1984). *Organizational Behavior: People and Processes Management.* Homewood, IL: Richard D. Irwin.

Frankl, V.E. (1997). *Man's Search for Meaning.* New York: Washington Square Press, Pocket Books, and Simon & Schuster.

Garmezy, N. (1991). "Resiliency and Vulnerability to Adverse Developmental Outcomes Associated With Poverty." *American Behavioral Scientist, 34*(4): 416–430.

Goleman, D. (2004, January). "What Makes a Leader (HBR Classic)." *Harvard Business Review,* 82–91.

Goleman, D., R. Boyatizis, and A. McKee. (2002). *Primal Leadership: Learning to Lead with Emotional Intelligence.* Boston: Harvard Business School Press.

Hammer, M., and J. Champy. (1993). *Reengineering the Corporation.* New York: HarperCollins.

Hultman, K. (1979). *Path of Least Resistance: Preparing Employees for Change.* Austin, TX: Learning Concepts.

Hultman, K. (1998). *Making Change Irresistible: Overcoming Resistance to Change in Your Organization.* Palo Alto, CA: Davies-Black Publishing.

Kepner-Tregoe. (1994). *House Divided: Views on Change from Top Management—-and Their Employees.* Princeton, NJ: Author.

Kotter, J.P., and L.A. Schlesinger. (1979). "Choosing Strategies for Change." *Harvard Business Review, 79*(3).

Kübler-Ross, E. (1997). *On Death and Dying* (reprint edition). New York: Simon & Schuster.

Kurzweil, R. (2001). "Law of Accelerating Returns." www.KurzweilAI.net.

Lawrence, P.R. (1969). "How to Deal With Resistance to Change." *Harvard Business Review, 69*(1).

Lewin, K. (1999, December 1). "Kurt Lewin: Change Management and Group Dynamics." *Thinkers.* London, England: Chartered Management Institute.

Lincoln, A., and R.P. Basler. (1953). *Collected Works of Abraham Lincoln,* volume 5. Piscataway, NJ: Rutgers University Press.

Manchester, W. (1983). *The Last Lion: Winston Spenser Churchill, Visions of Glory* (1st edition). Boston: Little, Brown and Company.

Mandela, N. (1994). *Long Walk to Freedom.* Boston: Back Bay Books.

Maslow, A.H. (1999). *Toward a Psychology of Being* (3rd edition). New York: John Wiley & Sons.

Maurer, R. (1996, June). "Using Resistance to Build Support for Change," *Journal for Quality and Participation.* http://www.findarticles.com/p/articles/mi_qa3616/is_199606/ai_n8735568.

O'Neil, J. (1993). *The Paradox of Success: When Winning at Work Means Losing at Life.* New York: Putnam and Sons.

Oestreich, D. (2001). *Our Star.* Redmond, WA: Author. http://unfoldingleadership.com/page7/files/ourstar.pdf.

Reivich, K., and A. Shatté. (2003). *The Resilience Factor: Seven Essential Skills for Overcoming Life's Inevitable Obstacles.* New York: Broadway Books.

Rotter, J.B. (1966). "Generalized Expectancies for Internal Versus External Control of Reinforcement." *Psychological Monographs,* 80(1, whole no. 609).

Russell, J., and L. Russell. (1998). *Managing Change.* Dubuque, IA: Kendall/Hunt Publishing Company for Credit Union National Association.

Russell, J., and L. Russell. (2003). *Leading Change Training.* Alexandria, VA: ASTD Press.

Rutter, M. (1977). "Protective Factors in Children's Responses to Stress and Disadvantage." In: M.W. Kent & J.E. Rolf (editors), *Primary Prevention in Psychopathology, volume III: Social Competence in Children.* Hanover, NH: University Press of New England.

Salk, J. (1973). *Survival of the Wisest.* New York: Harper & Row Publishers.

Schein, E. (1999). *The Corporate Culture Survival Guide.* San Francisco: Jossey-Bass.

Schein, E. (2001, July). Lecture at the Cape Cod Institute. Eastham, MA.

Schein, E. (2004). *Organizational Culture and Leadership* (3rd edition). San Francisco: Jossey-Bass.

Scott, C. (1995). Presentation at the 1995 Hunter Conference, Madison Area Quality Improvement Network. Madison, WI.

Senge, P. (1990). *The Fifth Discipline: The Art and Practice of the Learning Organization.* New York: Doubleday.

Skinner, B.F. (1938). *The Behavior of Organisms: An Experimental Analysis.* New York: D. Appleton-Century Company.

Solomon, R., and F. Flores. (2001). *Building Trust in Business, Politics, Relationships, and Life.* New York: Oxford University Press.

Spitzer, T.Q., Jr. (1996). *Managing the Human Side of Change.* Princeton, NJ: Kepner-Tregoe. http://www.quality.org/tqmbbs/prin-pract/peowise.txt.

Strebel, P. (1996). "Why Do Employees Resist Change?" *Harvard Business Review, 96*(5): 86–92.

U.S. Bureau of Labor Statistics. http://www.bls.gov/.

Webster's Encyclopedic Unabridged Dictionary of the English Language. (1996). New York: Random House.

Werner, E., and R. Smith. (2001). *Journeys From Childhood to Midlife: Risk, Resilience, and Recovery.* Ithaca: NY: Cornell University Press.

Additional Resources

Published Resources

Argyris, C. (1993). *Knowledge for Action: A Guide to Overcoming Barriers to Organizational Change.* San Francisco: Jossey-Bass.

Beer, M., and N. Nottria. (2000). *Breaking the Code of Change.* Boston: Harvard Business School Press.

Cohen, D.S. (2005). *The Heart of Change Field Guide.* Boston: Harvard Business School Press.

Gladwell, M. (2002). *The Tipping Point* (reprint edition). New York: Back Bay Books.

Hamel, G., L. Valikangas. (2003). "The Quest for Resilience." *Harvard Business Review, 81*(9): 52–54.

Harvard Business Review. (2005). *OnPoint Collection: Lead Change—Successfully* (3rd edition). Boston: Author.

Harvard Business Review. (2002). *OnPoint Collection: Organizational Resilience.* Boston: Author.

Holt, D., D. Self, A. Thal, Jr., and S. Lo. (2003). "Facilitating Organizational Change: A Test of Leadership Strategies." *Leadership and Organizational Development Journal, 24*(5): 262–272.

Kissler, G.D. (1991). *The Change Riders.* Reading, MA: Addison-Wesley Publishing Company.

Kotter, J.P. (1996). *Leading Change.* Boston: Harvard Business Review Press.

Kotter, J.P. (2002). *The Heart of Change: Real-Life Stories of How People Change Their Organizations.* Boston: Harvard Business School Press.

Luecke, R. (2003). *Managing Change and Transition* (Harvard Business School Essentials Series). Boston: Harvard Business School Press.

Quinn, R.E. (1996). *Deep Change: Discovering the Leader Within.* San Francisco: Jossey-Bass.

Scott, C.D., and D.T. Jaffe. (1989). *Managing Organizational Change.* Menlo Park, CA: Crisp Publications.

Senge, P. (1999). *The Dance of Change: The Challenges to Sustaining Momentum in Learning Organizations.* New York: Currency Books.

Organizational Resources

Organization Development Network, http://www.odnetwork.org/

ASTD's Organization Development and Leadership Community (ASTD membership required), http://www.astd.org/astd/resources/od_leadership_community/od_home

About the Authors

Jeffrey and Linda Russell are the founders and co-directors of Russell Consulting, headquartered in Madison, Wisconsin. For almost 20 years, the Russells have provided consulting and training services in such areas as leadership, strategic thinking and planning, leading change, employee quality of work life surveys, organization development, performance coaching, and performance management. Their diverse list of clients includes *Fortune* 500 companies, small businesses, social or nonprofit organizations, and government agencies.

Jeff Russell has a bachelor's degree of arts in humanism and cultural change and a master's degree of arts in industrial relations, both from the University of Wisconsin. He serves as an adjunct faculty member for that university, teaching for the small business development center, the Wisconsin certified public manager program, and a number of other certification programs with the University of Wisconsin campuses. He is a frequent presenter at local, state, regional, and international conferences.

Linda Russell has a bachelor's degree of arts in social work and has completed graduate work in rehabilitation counseling. She specializes in designing and implementing quality of work life surveys and in facilitating team and organization development interventions.

Jeff and Linda Russell have written five previous books, including *Leading Change Training* (ASTD Press, 2003) and *Strategic Planning Training* (ASTD Press, 2005). They also publish *Workplace Enhancement Notes,* a journal of tips for leading organizations.

With a company vision of helping create and sustain great organizations, Russell Consulting integrates theory, research, and real-world experience in its daily consulting and training practice. The Russells help their clients find practical management solutions to a challenging world that too often offers strategies that are long on hype and short on substance.

Readers wanting to know more about Jeff and Linda Russell and their work are encouraged to visit www.RussellConsultingInc.com or to send them an email at RCI@RussellConsultingInc.com. Please contact them if you have questions about the ideas in this book or would be interested in arranging for RCI's consulting or training services.